Thomas J. Quinlan

You Cannot Imprison the Word of the Lord!

June 12, 2005

Dear All:

As I commence my enforced but enthralling "retirement" I am filled with joy. I have the privilege of entering a new "career". I will finally have time to talk and to listen to people, As a workaholic and an ex-alcoholic I am going to have to change as never before, something I am always preaching to others.

History and especially Catholic Church history show and prove that all of life is filled with the simultaneity of Joy and Sadness. My joy is my new life: My sadness is the condition of the Church I still plan to serve. The sadness arises from:

1. The inability of OUR Church to continuously apply Gospel norms to its own life and the secular world it is supposed to compenetrate. This is manifested in"
    An hierarchical instead of an egalitarian Church
    A male one instead of an equal-gendered leadership
    Practicing the Ten Commandments instead of Jesus' commands
    Saving "souls" instead of establishing the Kingdom.

2. It is also manifest in our allowing ourselves to be engulfed in the Fundamentalistic Tsunami of the present aeon, precisely in the moment we had begun to extricate ourselves from our own fundamentalism and absolute-truth arrogance.
    Our turning back from the historico-critical method of Re-interpreting the Scriptures, the legacy of Paul VI
    Our continuing MIS-interpretation of the Genesis Myth which leads to dogmatic, moral, and spiritual aridity and error.

3. A stuck-in-the-thirteenth-century outlook on Natural Law which is the source of an antedeluvian attitude about the world and the flesh, and indeed of all reality.
    Undermining the spirituality of sexuality and marriage
    Eschewing ecology
    Crusading against Mother Science.

Two million people at the funeral or no, history will show that John Paul II was one of the worst Popes of the second/third millenium.

As I skip into retirement I am going to wake up every day, singing: 'HAPPY DAYS ARE HERE AGAIN'.

T.Q.

(Rev.) Thomas J. Quinlan

May 1, 1958 ~ June 13, 2005

YOU CANNOT IMPRISON THE WORD OF THE LORD

THOMAS JOSEPH QUINLAN, JR.
"TQ"

Ordained;
Sacred Heart Cathedral, Richmond, Virginia - May 1, 1958

Associate Pastor
Blessed Sacrament   Alexandria, Virginia
May 22, 1958 - January 26, 1963

Associate Pastor
Assumption   Keyser, West Virginia
January 27, 1963 - August 15, 1963

Associate Pastor
Sacred Heart   Norfolk, Virginia
August 16, 1963 - May 31, 1968

Pastor
Sacred Heart   Norfolk, Virginia
June 1, 1968 - December 6, 1968

Pastor
St. Vincent de Paul   Newport News, Virginia
December 7, 1968 - July 26, 1971

Pastor
Good Shepherd   Mt. Vernon, Virginia
July 27, 1971 - September 3, 1974

Pastor
St. Mary's   Norfolk, Virginia
October 1, 1974 - June 1, 1985

Sabbatical and Runaway from Bishop
June 1, 1985 - May 25, 1986

Founding Pastor
St. Kateri Tekakwitha   Tabb/Poquoson, Virginia
May 26, 1986 - June 11, 2000

Pastor
Church of the Holy Family   Virginia Beach, Virginia
June 12, 2000 - June 13, 2005

"There's just God and me and you. No devil. No angels.
But there is a heaven, and Jesus is in it.
And I can't wait to get there."

FIRST MASS
ST. MARY'S CHURCH,
WILLIMANSETT, MA.
MAY 4, 1958

We thought it would be most fitting,
while gathered at this sitting,
To eulogize our moderator--
better now than too much later.
May the first in Fifty-eight,
was truly a remembered date
We wonder how did Blessed Sacrament rate,
to get a cleric so celebrate.
Of escathological, he doth instruct us much,
of vigil lights at Mass and vestments and such,
he gets quite heated, we all perceive,
when some poor soul early from Mass does leave.
The plea "to get with it", we all do hear.
And yet, we are confused as to what IT is, I fear.
The Liturgical Movement--the "Deacons" at Mass
About Lay Participation he us does harass.
He's done a lot-(we're not sure what?)
For our Sodality, he's pepped us up--
He's bawled us out--He's mostly kept us running.
The poor young priest who gets the job
Of handling all these ladies--deserves a hand--a loud hurrah--
It's next to being in Hades!

1958 - Author unknown.

COVINGTON VIRGINIAN, TUESDAY AFTERNOON, JULY 16, 1968

Rev. Fr. Thomas J. Quinlan New Priest At Sacred Heart

The Rev. Fr. Thomas J. Quinlan, 37, formerly assistant priest at Sacred Heart Parish, Norfolk, has taken over duties at Sacred Heart in Covington, succeeding Fr. Joseph Jurgens who has retired after 29 years here.

Fr. Quinlan served in Norfolk for five years.

The Covington parish, where he officially began duties June 1, will be his first parish.

Prior to his assignme in Norfoldk, Fr. Quinlan served eight months as assistant priest at Church of the Assumption in Keyser, W. Va.

Earlier he served for five years as assistant priest at Blessed Sacrament Parish in Alexandria.

Fr. Quinlan was born in Springfield Mass., the son of Mr. and Mrs. Thomas J. Quinlan. He was educated at Saint Bonaventure Univeesity in Olean, N. Y. It was during his time at Bonaventure that he decided to enter the priesthood.

He was ordained at Sacred Heart Cathedral, Richmond, May 1, 1958.

He is presently serving as chairman of the Diocesan Religious Education Committee, chairman of Doctrinal Content Committee for Religious Education, and is a member of the Diocesan Liturgical Commission.

Fr. Thomas J. Quinlan
. . . First Pastorate

Members of St. Vincent de Paul Catholic Church pray during an Ash Wednesday service in Newport News on Feb. 9. The church was established in 1881, and the congregation was integrated in the 1970s when a Catholic church for black parishioners closed. PHOTOS BY SANGJIB MIN/DAILY PRESS

They're one family, with one Father

Parishioners say their diversity gives historic St. Vincent's in Newport News a youthful vitality.

BY JOY BUCHANAN
jbuchanan@dailypress.com | 247-4744

NEWPORT NEWS — Annette Murphy held up her conductor's baton and looked down at her sheet music for the song "A Joyful Ring."

"Ready? Bells up." She counted out a beat, "One, two, three, four."

Before her, about 10 women thrust brassy bells forward in time to Murphy's tapping on the music stand.

Ding-ding-ding, ding-ding-ding, ding-DING. Plunk plunk.

"Yes!" Murphy said. "That sounded wonderful."

It was the weekly Monday practice for the Freedom Ringers, a hand bell choir at St. Vincent de Paul Catholic. They counted their notes and tried to turn over their sheet music without stray dings of the bells.

In the room far to the left of the sanctuary, the class for new Catholics convened, waiting for soda and pizza before watching a video.

It was a typical night at St. Vincent's, but it might have been an unusual sight for visitors — there were black, Latino and white people in the class, and a mostly black bell choir led by a white director.

"It was an all white church, but now there's such a mixture," Murphy said. "It's warmer. It's like a big family."

The parishioners at St. Vincent's say it is the ethnic diversity that makes them feel at home, even though many of

Please see CHURCH/B2

St. Vincent de Paul Catholic Church in Newport News

SNAP FACT: Established in 1881, St. Vincent de Paul was the second Catholic Church on the Peninsula. The first, according to a timeline compiled by St. Vincent's, was St. Mary Star of the Sea at Fortress Monroe.

NOTABLE: The current building on 33rd Street in downtown, completed in 1916, is St. Vincent's second home. The first church building was completed in 1891 on Washington Avenue. Parishioners did most of the construction work.

St. Vincent member Mary Naylor, left, helps prepare lunches for the needy, while member Karin Geser, middle, greets church employee LeRoy Bunch at the church on Feb. 9.

Audrey Carr, left, and other members of Freedom Ringers of St. Vincent de Paul Catholic Church practice their music at the church in Newport News.

▶ CHURCH Continued from B1

Members appreciate diversity

them grew up in churches with homogenous congregations. As the church prepares for its 125th anniversary next year, the members are working hard together, caring for the church grounds, carrying on the church's charity missions and participating in regular church activities.

St. Vincent's was forced to integrate in 1970 when the local Catholic church for black people, St. Alphonsus on Marshall Avenue, closed. The black parishioners wanted nothing to do with the new church, resentful that their church was shut down, said Father Thomas Quinlan, who was St. Vincent's priest at the time of the merger. They also had worship and music styles different from the white church and didn't want to sacrifice them. Quinlan said the white parishioners weren't eager to integrate either.

"We're all equal, but you have to rub that in in the South," Quinlan said.

He said the merger went more smoothly than he'd expected. Quinlan left St. Vincent in 1971, but by then it was a comfortably integrated church. Today, it has about 260 member families and there is no predominant racial group, said Terri Simon, the church's pastoral facilitator.

"It's one of the most authentically integrated parishes in Virginia to this day," Quinlan said.

It was the cultural diversity that first brought Heather Livingston and her children to the church nine years ago. Livingston said her son John became friends with two classmates who attended St. Vincent's — one black, one Japanese and Italian. Livingston and her two children traveled from their home in Huntington Heights to visit the church and have attended ever since.

"In all my 52 years, this is the most diverse parish I've ever been too," Livingston said. "People don't care what you look like. They just want you to love God and help other people."

State Sen. Mamie Locke, D-Hampton, began her search for a church home when she moved to Virginia in 1981. Most of the churches she visited or attended for some time were predominantly white. After she visited St. Vincent in 1985, she stayed put. She said the sight of white and black people, Latinos and Asians, young and old —

From left, Evelyn Hartwell, Judy Otto and Evelyn Manely practice their music with other members of the Freedom Ringers of St. Vincent de Paul Catholic Church in Newport News on Feb. 7. PHOTOS BY SANGJIB MIN/DAILY PRESS

Church members Debbie Antinori, left, and Barbara Powell pray together after the Rite Christian Initiation of Adults class at the church in Newport News on Feb. 7.

> "In all my 52 years, this is the most diverse parish I've ever been too. People don't care what you look like. They just want you to love God and help other people."
> **HEATHER LIVINGSTON**
> church member

her cup of tea.

"From the very beginning, I felt welcome," Locke said. "It was more like my church back home in Atlanta. This was what I was used to and I found

In the church's Backdoor Ministry, the soup kitchen for the homeless, Kim and Dickie Spencer of Yorktown peel bananas for a fruit salad. The Spencers, who are white, have attended St. Vincent's for 14 years.

"Once we came here, we knew instantly this was it," Kim Spencer said. "Everybody brings their own thing to the table."

Like the gospel choir, a feature more typical of a black Protestant church than a traditional Catholic church. There's also the folk choir, the hand bell choir and a new children's choir. But might these activities just be a way to resegregate the congregation?

"No," Dickie Spencer said.

You Are Here
Locating interesting people and places across Hampton Roads

Each Tuesday, the Daily Press will take readers behind the scenes for a closer look at people and places of interest across Hampton Roads. If you know of a good story, tell us by calling (757) 247-4736 or by sending e-mail to fgaskins@dailypress.com.

each choir. They just have different sounds."

Elbow grease comes from many members of the church, too. Audrey Carr of Denbigh has attended the church since 1996. She said everybody helps out at St. Vincent's. The 83-year-old black woman is known to many in the congregation as "The Queen." She is an usher, member of the hand bell choir, and unofficial head of the "bucket brigade," a tiny group of older women who clean the church, even rubbing down the pews with Murphy's Oil Soap. Carr has been known to climb stepladders to scrub the Stations of the Cross along the sanctuary walls.

"I have never seen somebody walk by and not be friendly to others," Carr said. "It shows that there's no difference among us. We're all wor-

The Catholic Virginian

THE DIOCESE OF RICHMOND'S WEEKLY NEWSPAPER
Friday, August 8, 1969

Dress Rehearsal

The merged parish of St. Vincent's and St. Alphonsus, Newport News, has sponsored a summer program called Peninsula Progress. The program for inner-city children and adults included courses ranging from remedial reading to nutrition to sewing. Father Thomas J. Quinlan, tor, leads a rehearsal for the celebration of the Eu closing the summer program. (For more about Pen Progress, please turn to the center fold.)

13

For 1,000 Alexandrians, it was An Easter Excursion with the Risen Lord

The Catholic Virginian, April 26, 1974, Page 3

By Joan Fogarty
Special to The Catholic Virginian

The camaradarie began before they even got there. Occupants of big station wagons and little VW's finding their way through the 5 a.m. darkness up the George Washington Parkway from Mount Vernon, sensed that they were heading for the same place at this early hour on Easter Sunday morning. It wasn't a day for commuters — besides some of the suburbanites packed into their family cars recognized each other — and blinked their lights while the youngsters were beside themselves waving — they knew they were going to the same place alright — the Main Avenue Wharf in Washington.

There on the dock, with the huge excursion boat, "George Washington," of the Wilson Line looming behind him in the blackness, their pastor, Father Thomas J. Quinlan, wearing a white vestment embroidered with Christian symbols, was about to light the new fire from a charcoal brazier of hot coals.

HE WAS TELLING the crowd of more than 1,000 from Good Shepherd Church, that on the most sacred dawn of the entire year, they were gathered on the banks of the Potomac to take a journey in re-creation of the first Exodus of the Israelites. "By listening to His Word, by taking this pilgrimage, by eating the Easter bread, we climax our Festival of Hope. At this vigil-sunrise Mass, we can taste, touch, see, hear and feel the risen Christ — God's newest Creation — who is always present to His faithful people," he said. Gathered around him were his five co-celebrants.

The people's response, "Gonna put on my long white robe-down by the Riverside," echoed in song across the pier as the fire was lit. "With the Paschal candle as our new pillar of fire, let us board our ship for our journey of new hope and new life," he said.

It was a long line of people, (seemingly), not sleepy from their early morn awakening, but eager and full of anticipation, who walked through an arch of flowers and climbed the gangplank while a small brass band blared forth with "When the Saints Come Marching In." Everywhere the boat was decorated with paper garlands of flowers and the symbols of new life in bees and butterflies.

As they assembled — these celebrative people — in the second-deck main salon of the excursion liner, which normally plies the water carrying fun-seekers from the Capital City to Marshall Hall Amusement Park, they sang the antiphon, "All the earth proclaim the Lord, Sing your praise to God."

FATHER QUINLAN READ a Collect, called in the order of the Liturgy, "Exorcism of the Potomac." "Bless this river and purge it from the sewage of our sins," he intoned. "Cleanse it from the political corruption washing into it from both banks. Purify our beloved Potomac of its ecological diseases and sores. (One youngster later reported sighting 253 dead fish.) May our own celebration of the Easter mysteries initiate an age of national integrity and reverence for all Your elements. We ask this through the Risen Christ, Our Lord, Amen."

The new Paschal Candle was plunged into the water of the huge silver urn, used at Good Shepherd for Baptism by immersion, a three-fold Alleluia arose from the people, and the boat gave a mighty shudder as it left its moorings. An unofficial lookout cried out, "Heave-Ho!"

As Father Quinlan sprinkled hundreds of heads with Easter water, and the people renewed their Baptismal vows with resounding "We do's!" the shadows of the Fourteenth Street Bridge, the Washington Monument, and the city lights began to recede in the wake of the ship.

Exploring several Paschal themes in his homily, Father Quinlan dwelt on the reality of Chrsit's conquest of sin and death. "A human, Jewish, fleshy person appeared to believers. If we don't believe this, there is nothing to celebrate," he said. "He rose, He appeared, and He is actually present on this boat tonight — a living Sacrament by the water that surrounds us. The Easter bread, everything we experience, is the risen flesh of Jesus of Nazareth."

Both in age and attire, it was a divergent group he was addressing. There were the young, many in their patched jeans and survival jackets, like any other Sunday, others in mod slacks and coats or granny dresses topped with knit shawls; there were babies dozing in strollers and on parents' shoulders; there were men dapper in checks and plaids or casual in heavy Irish sweaters; there were matrons in stylish spring pants-suits and others in long dresses with fur stoles and orchids. An elderly lady wore a white straw hat and matching shoes and one pre-teen was in a real "Easter" dress and leghorn hat. But when the Rite of Peace came and they had the chance to wish each other a "Happy Easter," they moved as one, mingling together, warmly shaking hands, some seeking out special friends to kiss or embrace, as "Easter Parade" played somewhere in the background.

"CHRIST HAS DIED, Christ has risen, Alleluia," rang forth, as in the first gray light of dawn the liner slid past some Navy boats and under the Wilson Bridge. And as they rumbled on down the river, hundreds came forward to receive the Easter bread and wine. "Let us pause after receiving the new leaven of Eucharist," as the small children ran overhead.

Then up to the open top deck, the congregation marched behind the large Joy Cross, covered in daisies and Oriental bells. On all sides the grand old "George Washington" of the Wilson Line was shrouded in thick fog and Fort Washington on the Maryland side was discernible only by the lighthouse that guards its southern shore.

But the crowd didn't seem to miss the warm sunshine they had anticipated as they gathered in the open air for the Communion Meditation. The fog horn blasted its warning and a jet screamed toward National, but their voices boomed out over the Potomac, "Michael, Row the Boat Ashore, Alleluia!"

As the big boat nudged into its moorings at Mt. Vernon, there on the dock, beneath a cavernous arch representing the empty tomb, was a mass of Easter lilies. As the celebrant had earlier said "He has been raised, exactly as He promised."

The new Exodus was over and everyone was invited to partake of the Alleluia breakfast being served below. "Renewed in spirit, let us refresh our bodies," some celebrant said. And so they did — with fruit juices, sweet buns and lots of hot coffee.

And then it was everybody's boat as it headed back to port, to frolic or explore, to sit on the benches, look out at the fog and murky river and chat with friends; for young couples to stroll hand in hand along the decks or "frug" as the brass played on in the main salon, until they gathered before docking again for a short dismissal rite and final hymn of Thanksgiving, "Jesus Christ is Risen Today."

It seemed a happy, contented throng that disembarked. Said one, "We've been hearing 'The people are the Church. Buildings aren't the Church.' But, hey, maybe a boat is!!"

Photo by John Kendig

Worshippers Board For Vigil

Against the background of the pilot house on the excursion liner "George Washington," Father Thomas J. Quinlan leads his parishioners in the Communion meditation, the hymn "How Great Thou Art," during the Easter Sunrise liturgy on the Potomac River. (Photo by John Kendig)

15

Washington Star-News
Saturday, September 14, 1974

REV. TOM QUINLAN

The Liturgy of a 'Goodbye'

By Jack Hammett
Special to the Star-News

The Rev. Tom Quinlan of Good Shepherd Catholic Church in the Mt. Vernon area, who has led the way with enhanced liturgies in Northern Virginia, has been reassigned at his own request. After the Diocese of Arlington was formed this summer he felt irresistibly drawn to a ministry offered him by the Diocese of Richmond, to become pastor of St. Mary's in Norfolk, an inner-city, predominantly black community.

FATHER TOM, as most parishioners refer to him, was chiefly responsible for a liturgy committee that sought, and often achieved, in religious ceremonies the meaning behind today's culture overlaid on the sacred traditions of the past. The liturgical approach was accompanied by an ecumenical flavor.

The liturgies also reached youths at a time when routinely they seem turned off by formal religion.

When the Good Shepherd community reacted to his departure with consternation, he told them:

"No one of us is more important than another . . . . Each of you has a ministry to perform . . . . If this community of Good Shepherd is truly filled with Christ's love and with the Holy Spirit, the work we have begun together will continue to grow and prosper. It all depends on you!"

A SPECIAL "Goodbye" liturgy was celebrated upon his departure from the parish this week, with members of the clergy from nearby Christian churches participating.

Bob Mondlock, president of the community, said during the sermon, "We owe much to Father Quinlan for being the catalyst who brought us to this point. The community, of course, also can take credit for rising to the occasion and accepting the challenge. We must always keep in mind though, in true humility, our dependancy on God and how He has been the real driving force of our community."

As has been customary at Good Shepherd since Father Tom became pastor, the spirit of the liturgy was so strong that everyone was reluctant to go home. The committee had prepared for it, however. A family party was held immediately afterwards that gave way to a full-scale dance.

The people hadn't forgotten what he had been teaching them all along.

THE WONDERFUL CHURCH AND THE DAY THE "MAGIC DIED"

I remember the wonderful church and the day the "magic" died. But I'd rather remember when it was there!

Father Tom Quinlan was the pastor of Good Shephard. He insisted on being called Tom. Tom came to a parish made up of an affluent, mortgaged society people, made up of colonels, generals, congressmen and senators. Then there were those that were God fearing and God loving, set in traditional Catholic ways, that gave the community a balance of social, economic and education levels that few other parishes elsewhere in the country could claim.

We often prayed together as a new parish, in a little old white brick building that was called a church, hall, school, community building, parish house. The room was large and usually not too crowded, except on special days. The sliding doors often would be pulled closed to give the privacy needed for Sunday Masses. Even with the doors closed, parishioners filled in the back seats first and as the hall filled, additional areas were opened.

Little was available but a lot seemed to be possible. Tom's ideas transformed things so easily! We would work together, plan together, talk together, laugh together, pray together and often be chastised together through Tom's homilies. We understood everything with a clarity that eludes me now.

The song hymnal booklets were the first to go. Then the altar rail...then the kneelers...though each had its replacement in the new liturgy. The word that reached the parishioners was involvement. All aspects of the church came under the guise of involvement. Tom was always around. He challanged those saying the Rosary during Mass. He stared at those not singing during the entrance hymn or during the liturgy. He chastised those that left Mass early. Tom was often critical of the Pope, Bishop, parishioners, or any of his peer professionals that were not living up to the decisions of Vatican II. He was often critical of the old traditional ways but always showing initiative toward the new. Many could not tolerate his abusive language during the homily or his lack of tact in letting the pieces fall where they may in personal, frank discussions. Many wrote letters to the Bishop. Many walked out of Mass during his homilies and there were those that left the parish.

Meaningful involvement and innovation was the word of God through the New Liturgy, NOT through Tom. Family learning teams were initiated. Lay male and female ministers were appointed to distribute communion. A parish council was formed. Communion was taken by the hand. The Liturgy became meaningful through a lay committee. The Social Affairs committee worked on meaningful civic projects. The word involvement touched the lives of all parishioners and even those of the protestant faith that had their own parishes within our church community. The name of Good Shephard Parish reached across the United States whenever and wherever church people gathered to talk about the new Christian ways of worship.

But I remember the day the "magic" died. A new diocese was formed. Tom was transferred to a new parish. A new Bishop was named, and a new pastor appointed to Good Shephard. The Bishop and the new pastor gave new rules to follow. We missed Tom at first SWIFTLY and then subtly; our highly successful children's religious program was questioned, the adult speaker's lecture series was nearly cancelled, women were no longer given equal status as lay ministers, the plans for the new community church came under scrutiny, and the voice of the parish council was toned down by the new spiritual leadership.

But I remembered Tom and his "magic". I remembered his costume participation in the Octoberfest. I remembered the stagecoach and carousel at Christmastime. Who could forget the yellow volkswagon driven into church at Eastertime. I missed his calling us by our first names at Communion time. I missed the "magic" of his homilies...I missed Tom!

I hoped and prayed the "magic" Tom gave us would begin again...but it never did. Gradually I saw ourselves as we started drifting back into our old ways. I never asked anyone else if the "magic" died for them, I really didn't want to know! I'd rather remember when the "magic" was there, and I was just a small part of it!

"God be with you." "We shall overcome!"

Bill Bzpka
11-12-74

RELIGION

Closing a Clerical Show

Good Shepherd Church of Alexandria, Va., was once the embodiment of suburban Catholicism. The cavernous cinder-block building itself resembled a supermarket plunked down amidst an affluent neighborhood by some careless zoning board. The nine-year-old parish's membership list, drawn largely from the close-cropped and constantly changing ranks at the Pentagon and nearby Fort Belvoir, had initially been compiled from the local welcome-wagon files.

But then, three years ago, the parish got a new pastor. He was the Rev. Thomas J. Quinlan, now 42, an intense, long-haired, chain-smoking Moses who felt called to lead Good Shepherd's flock forth from institutional captivity. Quite orthodox as a young seminarian, he had grown to despise the way Catholics "divorced church from their daily lives." At Good Shepherd, he derided the complacent laity as "spiritual white trash" who merely dropped by church to fill up at God's "gas pump." Punctuating his sermons with words like damn, hell and bitch, he thundered against "gum-ball theology" and the "colonel syndrome" he found in both his parishioners and his superiors. He announced that he had come to purge "game-playing" Catholics and forge the parish into a legitimate community of faith. Some 150 outraged families walked out. Those who stayed were not only immersed in Quinlan's vision of community, but got season tickets for the zaniest liturgical show in town:

CHRISTMAS EVE MASS. Burlesquing the season's secular spirit, a procession of toys emerges from the sacristy; Teddy bears, dolls and soldiers move up the center aisle. Right in the middle of it all, decked out in spangles and waving a glowing magic wand, is the Blue Angel —Father Quinlan, of course. Santa Claus (an assistant priest) joins the march as it heads back toward the altar. Quinlan ducks out, then reappears in festive liturgical vestments, mercifully putting Christ back into Christmas.

PALM SUNDAY. Like so many undergraduates before homecoming, parishioners have put together floats and costumes for a parade around the church parking lot and right into the sanctuary. At the tail end comes a flower-festooned forklift truck; Father Quinlan, standing atop the truck's raised platform and waving a green branch, symbolizes Christ entering the Holy City.

EASTER. This time the Good Shepherd pastor gets his flock up at 4:30 a.m. to journey into Washington, D.C. There 1,000 parishioners and Episcopalian friends board a chartered excursion boat and float down the Potomac to celebrate the Resurrection with a sunrise Mass.

Behind the thunder from the pulpit and the theater at the altar, Quinlan had a serious purpose: galvanizing his tepid Catholics into self-starting Christians. He handed out generous doses of both responsibility and freedom. He appointed six women to distribute Communion and allowed worshipers to receive the home-baked Communion bread in their hands—contrary to the U.S. hierarchy's ban against the practice. His adult-education series became a standard stop on the religious Chautauqua circuit for speakers like Activist Priest James Groppi, Feminist Theologian Rosemary Ruether and assorted Protestant scholars. To help him lead his renewal, Quinlan expanded an embryo parish council into a vigorous 37-member body and hammered out programs with it in lively meetings that sometimes broke up at 1:30 a.m. Laymen, he counseled, "cannot be intimidated by crap." Despite the early defections, the parish managed to maintain its pre-Quinlan strength of some 750 mostly white, middle-class families as its fame attracted younger, more activist new members—some from towns an hour's drive away.

Following Orders. Four months ago, an administrative decision from Rome signaled the end of the parish's freewheeling days: the Holy See had carved a new diocese of Arlington out of the remote Richmond diocese, whose bishop, Walter Sullivan, had shown no interest in taming the maverick parish. Quinlan chose to remain under Sullivan's see; he landed in a mostly black inner-city parish in Norfolk, where he irrepressibly plans to continue as a spiritual *agent provocateur*.

Arlington's new bishop, Thomas J. Welsh, a solid traditionalist from Philadelphia, assigned an old-guard priest, Father John P. Hannan, 52, to take over Good Shepherd. After refusing at first to meet with the radicalized parish council, Hannan finally turned out for a meeting that drew 400 onlookers and occasioned catcalls, boos and some tears. "Were you sent down here to whip us into shape?" a layman demanded. Said Hannan: "I am just following orders." Just as briskly, he shelved or canceled many of Quinlan's programs and plans.

Last week Bishop Welsh himself visited the unhappy parish, some of whose members showed up wearing "smile" buttons upside down. Welsh insisted that he did not want to "wipe out enthusiasm" but seemed deaf to complaints about New Pastor Hannan. "We are talking on totally different levels," said one parishioner. "We told him we want to share in the ministry and not be just ministered to." Quinlan is confident that his former parishioners are now independent enough to carry on the struggle. "They are not fighting a local battle," he said in Norfolk. "They are part of the renewed church."

QUINLAN AS BLUE ANGEL AT CHRISTMAS

ABOARD FORKLIFT ON PALM SUNDAY
No gum-ball theology.

TIME, OCTOBER 21, 1974

Monday, Sept. 16, 1974 THE WASHINGTON

Classic Struggle Looms At Alexandria Church

By Marjorie Hyer
Washington Post Staff Writer

Grim-faced parishioners gathered in angry little knots after mass yesterday and tried to plot strategy in what is shaping up as a classic struggle between old-style authoritarianism and post-Vatican Council renewal in the Roman Catholic church.

The battleground is Good Shepherd church of Alexandria, the most progressive parish in the generally conservative new diocese of Arlington.

Under the leadership of the Rev. Thomas J. Quinlan, Good Shepherd had developed a reputation for deep involvement and decision-making by the lay members in everything from its building program to the parish's highly innovative liturgy and religious education programs.

When Father Quinlan left last week for a new parish in Norfolk, he was succeeded by the Rev. John P. Hannan, formerly of Queen of Apostles parish in Arlington.

In his first week at Good Shepherd, Father Hannan has:

• Ordered that the parish's six women lay ministers be removed from their duties. (Lay ministers assist in the distribution of the elements of the eucharist and may also administer communion to the sick. The Vatican has authorized both men and women to perform this function.)

• Ordered the archi-

See CHURCH, A8, Col. 3

Struggle Looming at Church

CHURCH, From A1

tect to stop work on the parish's million dollar building program, to which members have already pledged more than half the required amount and contributed $200,000.

• Put an end to the practice of communion in the hand—the practice whereby a member helps himself to the communion wafer instead of having it placed on his tongue by the priest or lay minister.

• Substituted a standard liturgy for the services tailor-made by the parish's liturgy committee.

• Challenged the church's long standing lecture series which this year includes such speakers as antiwar priest Daniel Berrigan and Dr. Rosemary Reuther, a theologian who has long been identified both with church renewal and with the feminist movement.

But what rankled members of Good Shepherd the most was not their new pastor's specific actions themselves, but the fact that he took them without consulting any lay leaders of the parish.

Jerry Sonosky, an attorney who is chairman of the finance committee of Good Shepherd, stood outside the church after the noon mass yesterday and talked about Father Hannan's actions.

Describing the parish as patterned after the directives of the Vatican Council that called for responsibility shared by laity and priest, Sonosky said that "the women in this parish are just flattened (by the removal of the six lay women ministers from the schedule).

"But the issue here isn't just the women, or the building program. The issue here is the whole question of renewal itself," he said.

"What he (Father Hannan) said to us was, 'Your by-laws are hereby abrogated.'"

Through its 37-member parish council and network of committees elected by the congregation, Sonosky explained, Good Shepherd has evolved a "system which has "wedded the decision-making role of the pastor to the advisory role of the congregation."

In his homily delivered at all four of yesterday's masses, Father Hannan said, "I know you have committees of the parish. I hope that you will understand that I am open to all advice and consultation.

"But I hope you will also understand that I have to make the final decisions and I'll just go ahead and make them — after I've heard the advice — and hope it will work out for the best interests of all of us."

At the beginning of his homily, Father Hannan acknowledged, "I have not talked to anyone except the other priests in the house (the church's rectory). I wanted to come to all of you at the beginning and tell you what my ideas are."

When reached by phone at the rectory yesterday afternoon for comment on the conflict building at Good Shepherd, Father Hannan refused to discuss future plans. "I'm busy now," he said.

Tom Gailliot, chairman of the lay ministers, expressed dismay over the treatment of the lay ministers.

"I feel he (Father Hannan) has picked something we have to challenge him on," said Gailliot. "We will challenge him under the knowledge that in the Gospel values we are all co-equals; we are all responsible; we are all priests to one another."

Good Shepherd, located in an area of $80,000 to $100,000 homes north of Mount Vernon, has a membership of about 750 families. A fair number of them come from outside the parish, drawn by the innovative programs of liturgy and religious education and by the strong sense of community the church has developed.

St. Mary's Radical Priest

Section J
Sunday, May 10, 1981

The Gospel According to Tom Quinlan

By JOHN COIT
Virginian-Pilot Staff Writer

HE LOOKS TIRED at noon Mass. Tall and gaunt. His face contains the ravaged expression of a man who just won't take care of himself. His voice, raspy and edged with an arch tone, echoes through the gothic confines of St. Mary's Roman Catholic Church on Chapel Street in Norfolk.

Father Thomas J. Quinlan, parish priest, eldest son of a New England Irish brood of 10, is about to offer Holy Communion. One by one the 15 or so faithful who come to this noonday rite step before him.

"Martha, the body of Christ. James, the body of Christ. Ernestine, the body of Christ. Here, friend, the body of Christ."

This done, the people return to their places. There is silence now. The sounds of traffic filter into the cool quiet of the church, which smells faintly of sandalwood and musty book covers.

Father Quinlan walks to a small lectern to the left of the people, following a lay reader's rendition of The Word. He begins to talk, his eyes down, a hand brushing a strand of hair from his forehead.

His homily has to do with Moses leading the Jews through the wilderness. He warms to it, telling of Moses' problems with his people, who had one crisis of faith after another, complaining of their miserable journey to the Promised Land.

No faith, says Quinlan. Just like the journey through life, through a Christian life. Got to have faith, got to keep up with The Word.

"Even with what they knew, with what Moses told them, they complained. Same kind of bitching you hear right in the parish. Thousands of people are falling away from the church. Good. Let them fall away. They never believed it anyway."

His homily done, he blessed the people.

"The Mass is ended, go in peace."

This noon lesson is just a glimpse at what the good father has up his sleeve. Quinlan's idea of a Christian life is far from the traveled road. In his view the church isn't a club, nor is it a place to tank up on a little soul food. It is where one of the most radical concepts in the history of man is taught and ordered spread.

"You got to love everybody, even jerks. And it's unlimited sharing. Every day, every year. All the time."

There's a ton of supporting information leading to that end, and T.Q., as he's known around St. Mary's, will do just about anything—from drive a Volkswagen down the center aisle to dress as The Blue Angel—to get the main message to his people.

"A priest, or any pastor, has one primary task," Quinlan says. "He has to preach the Word and celebrate the sacraments. And in that, he has to break the Word to the people so they understand just how radical the Gospel is."

So Tom Quinlan, a white priest with a black parish, who some people think is crazy as a loon, puts on the heavy dog each time he endeavors to make an idea 2,000 years old make sense to 20th-Century observers.

"When the culture starts to crumble, the church has to start on a new path, and we have to use a creative liturgy."

(See QUINLAN, Page J2)

21

Continued from Page J1

Since the mid-'60s, he believes, American culture has begun to crumble. And since Pope John XXIII's 1963 Vatican II Council, the Roman Catholic Church's great iceberg of tradition has also broken up.

"There's just God and me and you. No devil. No angels. But there is a heaven, and Jesus is in it. And I can't wait to get there."

The clipping from the newspaper morgue's file on Thomas J. Quinlan is yellowing. The date is May 16, 1964. The headline: "Debating Big Help, Young Priest Says."

There is a one-column picture of Quinlan looking very much like a priest of the Pat O'Brien variety: neat haircut, sensible eyeglasses, Roman collar, black jacket and vest.

He was assistant pastor of Sacred Heart Church then, and already formulating his ideas for a souped-up delivery of the Gospel. It was a time when the first cracks were beginning to appear in American culture, and T.Q. was itching to ride the flow.

"It is necessary for a priest to leave no areas of doubt when discussing matters of religion, morals and ethics. Debating disciplines a person to think clearly and to speak succinctly and positively."

There were other hints of the Tom Quinlan to come. He said then: "I used to take every advantage of seeing performances on the legitimate stage in the Washington area. Now I see the productions of Little Theater in Norfolk every chance I get."

This love of theatrics, stated early in his priestly career, says much about the pageants Quinlan would later produce to emphasize Christ's teachings. He insists his modern-day interpretations of the Scriptures are nothing new as a concept.

His old friend Father Robert E. French of Virginia Beach's Church of the Ascension, thinks Quinlan's style often obscures his scholarship.

"If anyone knows Father Quinlan, they know he is actually quite traditional. It's how he communicates. His style. Most people are not aware he is a classical scholar."

"Indeed, a conversation with Quinlan is a journey at warp speed through the ages—now to the 1st Century, next to the era of Greek metaphysical thinking, then to philosophies from the Councils of Trent, finally to the present, where he insists the Scriptures must be made understandable to modern man, that the old, rigid liturgical demonstrations of the past will not do.

"The church has always used theater to enhance the liturgy, to illustrate the Scriptures. The passion plays are an example."

He turned 50 in April, and it hasn't mellowed him much. He lights one cigarette after another, which may account for the rasp in his voice. Words come on air breathed through a throat nearly raw from constant inhalation of tobacco smoke.

He admits he smokes too much, probably doesn't eat right, and sleeps too few hours. "I haven't been to a doctor in years."

Quinlan is talking in the basement of St. Paul's Episcopal Church where he has kept a small bedroom and an office since the St. Mary's parish house, home for himself, another priest and several nuns, was destroyed by fire earlier this year. He is grateful for the generosity of his Episcopal brethren across St. Paul's Boulevard, and is fast to add with a slight twinkle: "Episcopalians aren't Protestants, anyway, you know."

St. Mary's, the oldest Catholic church in Virginia, is also one of the poorest. The destruction of the parish house was a particularly harsh blow to Quinlan, who lost most of his books.

Says French: "Catholic scholars and publishing houses think so much of his knowledge and insight they send him manuscripts and books to review. Much of that was lost in the fire."

"When I came to a black parish I was pretty happy. If I were to have a choice, I would serve a black parish or a parish in the mountains, where there are poor whites. I think that's the essence of Jesus' message. We have to always identify with the most oppressed people in society."

Quinlan has begun to razz those members of St. Mary's who are in the middle class and are not sharing their resources and time with the poor of the parish. "Middle-class blacks are just like middle-class whites. Race isn't the issue, it never has been the issue, really. It's class."

He adds, "I'm starting to get on 'em about it, too. If the people in this parish are beginning to think this is a club, then they better think again."

Eric K. Brown, the Parish Council president, says there is much affection for Quinlan, although some parishioners are not comfortable with his theatrical style.

"Personally, I like it. It helps us understand the Word of God."

On Quinlan's other point, he adds: "Classism and racism are so closely tied, aren't they? A lot of the oppression that occurs today is of an international scope. But Father Quinlan is certainly a theological historian and scholar. He knows what he's talking about."

Quinlan said one of the things he wants for St. Mary's is a black priest, but there are only two in the Diocese of Richmond.

Says Brown: "A black priest would be good, especially as a role model. It would be nice if we could see a black face at the altar. But what color a man's skin is shouldn't be as important as if he's a good Catholic and a good Christian."

One member of Quinlan's parish, a convert in her late 50s, says: "I hate for T.Q. to get talking, 'cause when he does he makes you feel like you ain't done nothing for nobody. But he live it. He live it everyday and the people know that."

The nuns who lost their rooms and possessions in the fire have been moved into public housing, keeping with their vows of poverty. It's a tough part of town.

Says Quinlan: "The people will protect them."

He cuts almost no slack. He recently railed against the behavior of some of the parish young, telling parents that their children were acting like a "bunch of black brats."

However, when he ran a white, middle-to-upper-class parish in Alexandria he called them "spritual white trash" because they would not heed what he calls the "radicality" of the Gospel.

To underline his feeling that social justice is a holy obligation, he has vocally supported the plight of 54 female workers struggling for better pay and benefits at St. Mary's Infant Home, a private sanctuary for mentally and physically handicapped children. The home has a board of trustees composed of lay people, many non-Catholic. Quinlan, as pastor of St. Mary's, is one of the 24 board members. The home is no longer connected, officially, to the church.

Quinlan chortles when he reveals that some board members wrote a note to board chairman Bishop Walter Sullivan, head of the Richmond Diocese, "asking him to silence me. They don't know the bishop very well."

Indeed, Quinlan's controversial statements from the pulpit, and his flashy theatrics when teaching the Gospel, might have drawn more than a little fire from a less tolerant See.

"Tom Quinlan has been the scapegoat for a lot of priests and a lot of Catholics who maybe would like to be doing what he's doing but don't possess his grasp of the issues nor his smarts," French says, then adds, "Quinlan has an honesty that is total. If he has a real fault, it's using that honesty too bluntly. He's not very diplomatic."

"If you wonder how I survive, it's because of my Bishop. And good friends, and my study of the Scriptures," Quinlan said. "We know so much more now about what the Scriptures mean, how they should relate to the present state of humanity."

Bishop Sullivan says Quinlan has "brought a real vitality to St. Mary's, a presence of the church into the black community. He is respected by both Catholics and non-Catholics."

He added: "Father Tom Quinlan is actually quite orthodox in his beliefs. Yes, he has been a leader of renewal. His style is unique, nobody can duplicate it, and nobody will. He has more baptisms, funerals and weddings than any other priest in this diocese."

His antics are legendary. Last Easter he dressed as Superman and had the altar surrounded by a cardboard Metropolis. The script, written by two members of the liturgy committee, was supposed to parallel the Gospel according to Mark.

"The apostles," Quinlan said at the time, "wanted a Superman, just like all their descendants. They didn't want a Messiah who said you got to suffer and die and all that."

The Superman figure, eventually, stands helpless, while a powerful Jesus, portrayed by a young black boy, a humble carrier of The Daily Planet, defeats the evil Lex Luthor.

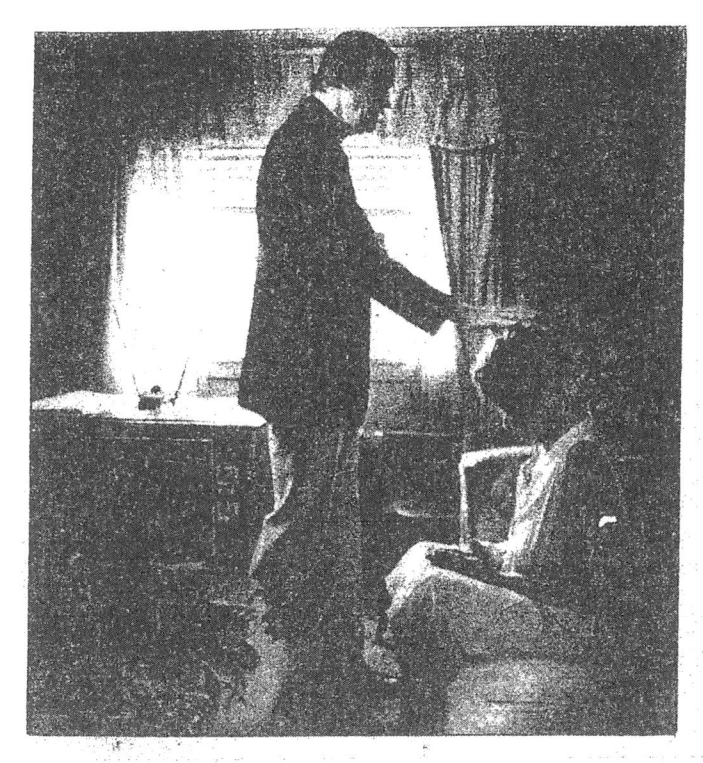

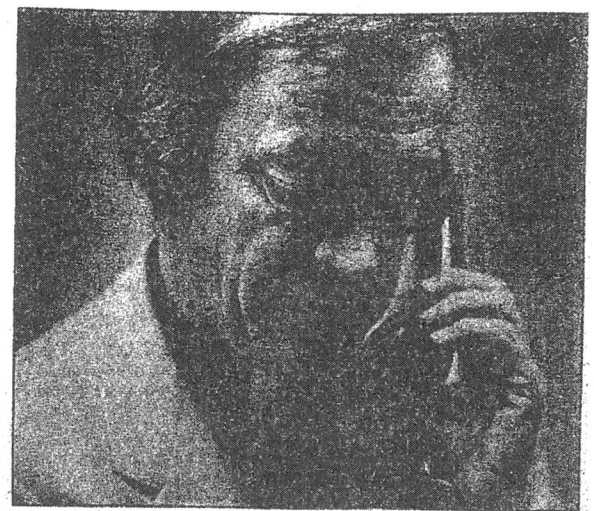

"There's just God and me and you. No devil. No angels. But there is a heaven, and Jesus is in it. And I can't wait to get there," says Father Thomas Quinlan, pastor of St. Mary's Catholic Church. At left, he gives Communion to Corrine Parker at her Lincoln Street home.

Staff Photos by Rob Kinmonth

In 1984, Quinlan's 10-year tenure as St. Mary's pastor will be over. He will have to move, which is church regulation.

Before he leaves, he says, "I'd like to develop the school. I would like to redecorate the church, although I wouldn't want somebody coming in and bastardizing one of the most beautiful, gothic churches in the South."

His days are spent following pastoral duties, from giving Communion to a shutin, to comforting the sick and giving last rites to the dying.

When he can get away, which isn't often, he and other priest friends go to Nags Head and a house in Southern Shores, "which we bought when you could still buy a place for $16,000."

Asked for a bit of favorite Scripture, Quinlan immediately takes out a large red Bible, and turns to the Gospel according to John, Chapter 20, Verses 30 and 31.

"Now Jesus did many other signs in the presence of the disciples, which are not written in this book; but these are written that you may believe that Jesus is the Christ, the Son of God, and that believing you may have life in His name."

This Easter, taking a newspaper article about ships standing idle in the harbor, their captains faced with a web of red tape, Quinlan and his liturgy committee devised a script showing a parallel between a ship captain's navigating the obstacles of the harbor and a Christian's struggle to reach a Christ-like existence.

And there was Quinlan, dressed as a captain, in Naval officer's hat and coat, facing a literal web of red tape, while a parishioner representing Jesus stood on the other side.

Each parishioner was then asked to write out the obstacles keeping him from a Christian life, these slips of paper to be passed to the Jesus figure.

"If you came off a Greek collier and walked into the church you might think all this is some sort of gimmickry, trick. But the parishioners have been informed of what's coming, and what it means, and how it relates to Scripture. For too long we've had a churchy world and a secular world. We've got to bring the two together if the Scriptures are going to make any real sense."

Quinlan was born in Springfield, Mass. He didn't go to Catholic schools, and he is the only one of the 10 Quinlan children to enter religious life. He attended seminary at St. Bonaventure in Olean, N.Y., and quit that twice, working for a railroad and a sporting goods factory before returning and taking his vows.

Ordained in 1958, he was first assigned as an assistant parish priest in Alexandria. From 1963 to 1968 he was assistant pastor at Sacred Heart in Norfolk before going to Newport News, then back to Alexandria.

When he left Alexandria to come to St. Mary's in 1974, he left behind a white, middle-class parish that had been totally transformed, from a traditional Catholic community to one that was astir with Quinlan's renewal ideas, so much so they were in conflict with the priest who replaced him and the bishop in Northern Virginia who wanted a slower transition from old values.

The flap made Time magazine, was brought to the attention of the Holy Father in Rome, and Quinlan found himself a celebrity as he took the reins at St. Mary's.

Since coming here, the parish has expanded by three times, to 1,500 members, 90 percent of them black, many from inner-city neighborhoods in Norfolk's project housing. The church has a school, all black, and since Quinlan took over, St. Mary's has a first-rate Gospel choir, which Quinlan proudly believes can lock horns with any traditional black Protestant Gospel choir around.

He has brought black art and culture into the church, and says: "A lot of the people thought they had to be de-blackized so they could get Romanized. No. The church has to adapt to the people. They are the church."

As he has at his other parishes, Quinlan insists that the Parish Council be equal with its pastor. He admonishes his people to minister to each other and in their community at large. He brings in Protestant preachers for revivals. This year he has invited The Rev. Dr. John Bryant of Bethel African Methodist Episcopal Church in Baltimore to lead one.

He openly defies Papal decree on some issues.

On birth control: "It's up to the conscience of the couple."

On premarital sex: "I don't know what it adds to a relationship, but it's a minor sin."

On homosexuality: "The tradition of anti-homosexuality goes back to Moses, when he had to kick the prostitutes, male and female, out of the temple. Any homosexual, however, has as much right to sit in the front pew and worship God as a married, heterosexual person. I can never see the day when a homosexual marriage could be performed in the church, because they cannot reproduce. But I can see a time when a relationship between two people might be blessed. Because of what they are, they shouldn't be cut off from their church life."

On priestly marriage and the ordination of women: "I'd like to get married, but at this point I don't know who'd have me. And yes, I think women should be priests, absolutely. It would change the entire church."

On such things as being born again; is he? "Sure, 15 million times."

The Catholic Virginian
serving the people of the diocese of richmond

BER 20, 1980

Workers Backed

Father Thomas J. Quinlan leads parishioners of St. Mary's Church, Norfolk, in prayer during a demonstration in support of striking workers at St. Mary's Infant Home, across the street from the church. The workers, many of whom live in housing projects in the neighborhood and some of whom are parishioners of St. Mary's, went on strike Oct. 5 in an attempt to force the infant home management and board to bargain with them through their union. Norfolk's six Catholic pastors have joined Bishop Walter F. Sullivan in a statement supporting the workers.

The Catholic Virginian, June 3, 1977

Complainers Should Be Open to God

Editor, The Catholic Virginian:

I write in reference to all the complainers who can't seem to cope with Father Thomas Quinlan's liturgies. If Father Quinlan's type of liturgy seems to turn you off, you should have consulted him and asked him to explain. Evidently you didn't understand it. That would have been the most adult way to go about it.

Our Lord and Savior, Jesus Christ, must be very happy with Father Quinlan's work. The membership (at St. Mary's, Norfolk) has grown from 184 to 519 families.

These complaints are serving only one purpose: to bring about disunity within the ranks of God. Don't be surprised. The devil goes to church, also . . . .

I have attended Mass at St. Mary's and have also met Father Quinlan. I have no complaints. We need more priests like him. I also was really overwhelmed listening to St. Mary's Gospel Choir. Why not compliment on some of the good things that Father Quinlan has done? In our own self-righteousness we tend to forget that God is no respecter of persons, be they complainers or non-complainers.

Just suppose the Catholic Church worshiped God like the Jews did in the Old Testament? They lifted up their hands in holy praises, and clapped their hands. David leaped and danced in the presence of the Lord . . . .

Now Communion in the hand, why not? There are some who are against it. When Jesus blessed and broke the bread, He said "take and eat." I haven't seen any Scripture stating that Jesus placed a particle of bread on each of the apostles' tongues.

Personally, I think the Holy Spirit is removing a lot of man-made laws that have been implemented in the Church down through the centuries. Now the Holy Spirit is preparing the Bride for the Groom. When Pope John XXIII said he was going to open the windows and doors of the Church to let in some fresh air, that fresh air is none other than the Holy Spirit and He is renewing the Church with new changes in our form of worship to make it more livelier and more alive. Jesus Christ is risen. That is something to shout and rejoice about and also something to get excited about. When you go to church on Sunday you are already supposed to have God in your hearts; so carry Him everywhere you go . . . .

So all of you complainers and those who are against renewal, be open to the will of God. He will bring you through the storm. There is a brighter day ahead. As Christians, we are all one in the Body of Christ. Don't give the evil one a chance to break the body down and cause disunity.

Lester Smith
Portsmouth

'Reverence, Pride, Manners' in Style

Editor, The Catholic Virginian:

After reading about Father Quinlan's fork lift ride during Mass and Father Pat Apuzzo calling anyone who objects "hypocritical," I might as well get into the act (pardon the pun).

In the first place, black Americans are educated and they don't need to be treated like children. They are quite capable of attending a normal Mass, grasping the gospel message, keeping the faith without being talked down to. I think the old phrase is don't insult my intelligence, please.

Second, I wonder why millions of Catholics have attended Mass through the years faithfully and they never had a fork lift to guide them? I cannot help but wonder how all those good people kept the faith, went off to fight holy wars for the Church and never once saw Father Quinlan's show. Surely Father Apuzzo is not comparing Quinlan to St. Francis' religious plays? I read about Catholics fed to the lions in Rome, rather than denounce their faith; they never saw Father Quinlan's fork lift ride. Where did the faith come from?

Some of the innovators are not following Vatican II but they call *us* names because we balk at dressing up like cabbages. They would have us believe unless we follow them and join the street jargon, nitty-gritty, the Catholic Church is going to fall down and we do not have faith in God. Baloney.

I am reminded of the story of the emperor's new clothes. No one had the courage to say he wasn't wearing any. Have courage and speak up and don't leave the Church. It is your Catholic duty to speak up.

If it is hypocritical to ask if this bus is going to heaven or if this bus is going to Basin Street East, then call me anything you want to. I didn't think good manners, dignity, reverence and pride in one's religion had gone out of style in the '70s just 'cause I don't boogie.

Thelma K. Jones
Norfolk

Why 'Berate' Questioners?

Editor, The Catholic Virginian:

Using methods with time-honored traditions in the Church, Father Quinlan and others, according to Father Pat Apuzzo, have done wonders in "putting flesh on a once-lifeless and ossified ritual." What an inspiration to have the Eucharist described in such glowing terms by a man of God. What a wonderful description of the greatest *living* example of our faith.

Is it any wonder that they who have converted to Catholicism find themselves in such a bewildered and confusing state of mind? How strange it must feel to be chastised and berated for daring to question the "shock tactics" being used and witnessed in some of our churches today. If such modern day promotions of motorcycles, fork lift, helicopters and offensive language have such time-honored roots in the tradition of the Church, what caused such a deterioration in the Holy Sacrifice of the Mass that it became a "lifeless and ossified ritual?" Surely, after such lengthy use of theatrics, wouldn't the opposite of the foregoing be true?

The Church truly cries out for unity and healing and Father Apuzzo is right when he says respect of persons and charity for others are requisites in order to bring this about. Maybe, just maybe, if Father Quinlan stopped using offensive language he would be easier to listen to and maybe, just maybe, if Father Apuzzo was more sympathetic to the needs of others, he might be able to do a little listening himself.

Thomas F. Murphy
Suffolk

Parishioner at St. Mary's plays the role of Nat Turner on Ash Wednesday

Slave's life provides basis

for masses

Staff photos by Michele McDonald

Philip Lucas plays the part of Nat Turner, the slave who led a rebellion, in a re-enactment of Turner's trial in Southampton County by parishioners of Norfolk's St. Mary's Catholic Church.

By APRIL WITT
Staff Writer

NORFOLK — Father Thomas Quinlan, the man who brought Darth Vader and the Wizard of Oz into the sanctuary, is at it again.

Quinlan, the white pastor of the 98 percent black St. Mary's Catholic Church, is basing his masses for this liturgical year on the life of Nat Turner. Turner led an 1831 slave revolt in Southampton County in which dozen of whites and blacks were killed.

"You can't get 'Rootsier' for the Afro-American," Quinlan said. "You can't get more into black culture in America than to reflect on the meaning of the Nat Turner insurrection."

Studying Turner, he said, also emphasizes a central tenet of Christianity because the slave, like Jesus, believed his mission was to liberate his oppressed people.

"Except for the violence, it's just a perfect parallel to Jesus," said Quinlan, whose fondness for calling things as he sees them has earned him a reputation as a lovable, bad-boy priest.

In masses throughout Advent and Lent, St. Mary's parishioners have dramatized segments of Turner's life — from his secretly learning to read the Bible as a child, to his young manhood, when he believed God told him to lead a slave revolt.

As the drama nears its Easter close, Quinlan, with the finely honed theatrical sense of a Broadway producer, has decided to take his show on the road.

Palm Sunday, when other Catholic masses will be based on the trial of Jesus in Jerusalem, Quinlan and a busload or two of parishioners will go to Courtland to re-enact Turner' historic trial there.

During the revolt, Turner was joined by about 75 other slaves. They roamed through Southampton County, killing about 55 white people.

The slaves were headed for Courtland, then called Jerusalem, when their revolt was put down by white troops. Afterward Turner was tried and hanged in Courtland, the Southampton County seat about 50 miles west of Norfolk.

To some people, Quinlan said, tying Turner's revolt to religious worship and the life of Jesus is shocking.

"Some are upset by it. Some parishioners oversimplify it by just going around saying he murdered people.

"Some don't want the challenge," he said. "It's such a painful facet of the past that they don't want to think about it."

But to Quinlan — who has spent much of his career challenging his parishioners and cutting a creative swath through the Catholic liturgy — it is just business as usual.

In a middle-class Alexandria parish he served in the early 70s, Quinlan made a point about the commercialization of Christmas by asking his parishioners to dress like giant toys on Christmas Eve.

At St. Mary's, where Quinlan has served since 1974, he has based liturgical years around, among other things, "Star Wars" with Darth Vader as the devil, and the Broadway musical "The Wiz."

"The Wiz, that was gorgeous," Quinlan said, laughing deeply as he recalled the riotous paths down which he has led his willing flock. "You wouldn't believe it. We had 2,000 yellow bricks in the main aisle — it was beautiful.

"We had all those people who could sing and dance, and at Easter Vigil you got to the Emerald City, to heaven."

Of his unorthodox ways, Quinlan said: "My parishioners presume I'm crazy anyway, so I get away with murder."

Despite the theatrics and controversy, Quinlan's primary goal remains to teach his charges.

"I try to get them to think about the message instead of reading some 2,000-year-old boring book called the Bible, you know," he said.

By using modern themes to illustrate the liturgy, people "get the human connection," Quinlan said.

"Once they get that, they really get into it. They don't treat Jesus as some kind of floating spirit."

The emphasis on Turner this church year has really hit home for Quinlan's congregation, he said.

"It's one of the best and the toughest we've ever done," Quinlan said. "The implications are unbelievable, and you don't have to stretch your imagination much — I mean, you can almost smell Courtland from here."

The lesson he hopes everyone in the parish will come away with, Quinlan said, is that all Christians are called to be liberators.

"Christianity is radical," Quinlan said. "And the fact is, Jesus is our main liberator; he liberated us from sin and oppression.

"All Christians today are called to liberate others just as Turner tried, against all odds, to liberate black Americans' ancestors — just like at St. Mary's soup kitchen we try to liberate people who are just sitting around on the street and not eating nothing."

Quinlan conceded that Turner's use of violence complicates his use as a Christian role model.

"The violence is the delicate part," Quinlan said. "He selected the wrong method to achieve his goal — that's all we can say. We don't condone it, but we can't make a moral judgment. We're not in that desperate situation."

At the Ash Wednesday evening mass, Quinlan spoke of Turner's belief that he was destined for greatness.

"That was some statement for a black slave to make 153 years ago," he told the parishioners. "That was saying, 'I am somebody' and 'black is beautiful' long before the first slaves were freed.

"Turner was a man with an unbelievable vision of freedom," Quinlan said as he stood beside a wood and paper rendition of a slave shack erected in the sanctuary.

"Somehow he knew — I don't know how — but somehow he knew that Jesus died on the cross so every man and woman could be free," Quinlan said, and a sea of black faces nodded back at him.

On Good Friday the liturgy committee is planning an African funeral dance for Turner, Quinlan said. At some point, Quinlan hopes to arrange for his congregation to don chains, which they can then throw off at an appropriate moment in the service.

"Getting black people to wear chains would be very heavy," he said.

Brother's keeper

Church offers a hot meal in hard times

By SHARON COLEMAN
Compass Staff Writer

In response to the area's high unemployment, St. Mary's Catholic Church last Monday opened its own soup kitchen, the first of its kind for the nearly 200-year-old parish.

The soup kitchen, in the cafeteria of nearby St. Mary's Academy, offers a day's meal to the parish's elderly and unemployed.

The Rev. Thomas J. Quinlan says the kitchen fills an immediate need of the community.

"The number of people applying for food at the door and asking for sandwiches has quadrupled since December," Quinlan said.

Tidewater's unemployment rate was nearly 7 percent then; today, it's more than 8 percent.

"Also," Quinlan said, "some people that you give canned food to have no place to cook it," so the church decided to open a kitchen.

Catholic lay persons, who wish to remain anonymous, contributed $7,000 for the food. St. Mary's Infant Home, a nearby but unrelated institution, donated $1,000 and the church spent $700 of its own for pots and pans.

Quinlan said he had hoped to open the kitchen in January, but had to postpone the start because of unexpected delays, such as the need for a zoning variance allowing the church to serve food to the public and a new stove hood required by city health inspectors.

So far about 30 parishioners have volunteered to serve and prepare the food at staggered intervals. Among them is Lula Scott Wilson, manager of the soup kitchen.

Aided by her husband, James, a merchant seaman, and her mother, Alice Swinson, she can be found nearly every day at the soup kitchen, managing the food pickups and selecting the day's menu.

On Monday and Tuesday of the first week of operation, the soup was chicken and rice. Wednesday and Thursday, beef stew was served. Friday, Navy beans with ham hocks, hot dogs and rolls — all homemade — were on the menu.

Mrs. Wilson, a converted Catholic who recently left the labor force, said she finds her work in the soup kitchen very rewarding. "I love it," she said. "I've always wanted to do things like that. I love doing for people, such as the elderly and the shut-ins."

The kitchen is open Mondays through Fridays, from 1 p.m. to 2 p.m. Most of the people are senior citizens who supplement their Social Security income with the meals, Mrs. Wilson said. A few are young, recently unemployed men and a few are drifters.

> "The number of people applying for food at the door and asking for sandwiches has quadrupled since December."
>
> The Rev. T.J. Quinlan

As many as 60 people have been served at one sitting, she said, and most have become regulars.

"Most come every day," Mrs. Wilson said, "but each day, you get new ones."

They start drifting in about 1 o'clock. Small bands of neatly dressed senior citizens, mostly women, take their places along the aluminum benches. It is somewhat of a social hour for them, and they often can be seen waving to acquaintances and chattering away about the day's events. A woman sitting alone a couple of benches away is asked to join the crowd.

"Q.T. sent a letter," one of the women said, referring to Father Quinlan's bulk mailing informing all Tidewater Park residents of the soup kitchen. "He's always trying to do something to help the people."

Jerome Jones is a young, unemployed man who "found out through a friend" about the free meal. Friday was his fourth day at the kitchen, and he says the high rate of unemployment makes more such kitchens a necessity.

A resident of Young Park, Jones is divorced and has been jobless for six months, he said. He used to be a truck driver for North American Van Lines here, but was laid off. Since then, he has been in and out of the employment lines, he said, adding: "It's a good thing I'm by myself at the moment."

Kermit Seldon found out about the soup kitchen from a memo on the Union Mission's bulletin board. Seldon, a middle-age man, is a laid off merchant seaman. Three and a half months of unemployment have left him looking a little worn. A native of Newport, R.I., he was a chief cook stranded here when he couldn't find work aboard another vessel.

"I'm trying to get out (from unemployment), but Mr. Reagan cuts us out from the funds," he said of the president's domestic policies.

According to the recent unemployment figures, widespread layoffs and plant closings pushed the nation's jobless rate to 9 percent last month — a figure last reached during the height of the Arab oil embargo. The labor force was smaller then, so the number of people out of work was smaller.

Currently, there are 9.9 million Americans out of work. Included in Tidewater's labor force of 338,000 are 27,600 unemployed. Joblessness among adult males, traditionally the family breadwinners, has increased significantly; so, too, has unemployment among blue-collar workers and blacks. Seldon fits all three categories.

"I think we need more places like this," he said, taking a sip of his only meal for the day. "I think we need some for seven days a week, as hard as a dollar is."

Church Kitchen Draws Many For Free, Hot Meal

NORFOLK (UPI) — Harkening to the days of the Great Depression, a downtown Catholic church has opened a soup kitchen to feed the needy.

"A lot of the older people who come in here say this is just like the Depression," the Rev. Thomas Quinlan, pastor of St. Mary's Church, said.

"It's a sad, sad indicator of the times when we have to open a soup kitchen. This is a depression, as far as I can tell, and maybe we should admit it."

Since the kitchen opened in St. Mary's school March 29, 30 to 50 people have stopped in between 1 and 2 p.m. daily for a lunch of hot soup and a sandwich.

"We wait on people, instead of having them go through a line," he said. "Going through a line isn't very Christian, I think."

The people who are served Monday through Friday in the church's soup kitchen "generally are those who've lost Social Security benefits or food stamps," Quinlan said.

"The idea came about after so many people started coming to the door asking for food. But what good are canned goods if you don't have a place to cook them? So we opened the kitchen."

Lulu Wilson comes in early daily to make "real soup, not stuff out of a can," Quinlan said.

Her husband James helps her, and another six volunteers staff the kitchen and serve food.

During its first two weeks of operation, the kitchen served chicken and rice, beef stew, beans with ham hocks, hot dogs and rolls — all homemade.

"We would have opened in January, but we had to have health inspectors and fire inspectors in first," Quinlan said. "I know we would have had a lot more people coming in during this bad winter if we'd been open."

Catholic lay persons in Norfolk and around the state have donated $7,000 for the soup Quinlan said enough donations had been given to keep the kitchen open.

Quinlan said the soup kitchen's clientele includes a lot of lonely "older folks" seeking companionship, unemployed men and an occasional "wino."

The soup kitchen also serves as the cafeteria for the school children.

"The kids sponge off the tables and sweep their classrooms at night, because they know the poor people come in here for meals after they finish theirs," he said. "They're very good about keeping the place clean."

Daily Press, Sunday, May 2, 1982

Quinlan began soup kitchen

I have never been hungry in my life, thank God. And one thing I could never stand is to see some person or animal hungry in a country so full of riches. My vote for a good neighbor goes to the Rev. Thomas Quinlan at St. Mary's Catholic Church for establishing the soup kitchen.

I never met him, but he makes for a good neighbor by taking action instead of words.

F.D. O'Toole
Mason Creek Road

The Catholic Virginian, May 3, 1982

Soup kitchen's aid, need increase

The word has spread about the soup kitchen being run by St. Mary's parish in downtown Norfolk. Father Thomas J. Quinlan, pastor, says that as a result of a United Press International wire story, he received a check from Montana and another from Massena, N.Y.

In addition, a story in a Northern Virginia paper brought some donations from that region. And in Tidewater, he said, individuals continue to show their compassion for the poor. He recently received a check for $700, he said, from a man in South Norfolk.

Attendance at the meal, served Mondays through Fridays from 1 to 2 p.m., has continued to grow. The single-day high last week was 137. The large parish hall is well able to accommodate a large turnout, he said, but the church could use more volunteers to prepare and serve the meal of homemade soup and sandwiches.

St. Mary's is located in an area of public housing projects, and the soup kitchen is designed primarily to serve the people who live in them.

WEST SIDE

St. Mary's keeps on feeding the hungry

Church kitchen has been serving poor 10 years

By Charlene Cason
Correspondent

Robert, 31, is a homeless, unemployed roofer. When he has money, which isn't often, he buys food. When he doesn't, he eats lunch at St. Mary's Catholic Church.

St. Mary's Soup Kitchen celebrated its 10th anniversary last week. One of a handful of church-operated kitchens, it serves free, hot lunches four days a week to anyone who can't afford a meal.

"When I was working, this was the furthest thing from my mind," said Robert, who asked that his full name not be used. "If I have a few dollars, I won't take that bowl from someone else."

Robert has family in the area, but said pride prevents him from asking for their help. He eats at other area soup kitchens, but finds the food at St. Mary's good and nutritious.

He was embarrassed the first time he ate at a soup kitchen, but "when you're stomach's growling, you got to let pride get out of the way," he said.

St. Mary's soup kitchen ministry was begun by the Rev. Thomas J. Quinlan, pastor at the church in 1981. Not many people came in the first weeks. Today, 80 to 200 men, women and children eat there Mondays, Wednesdays, Thursdays and Fridays.

"The Peace and Justice Committee started the soup kitchen because the need was obvious," Quinlan said. "People were coming to the school kitchen, asking for food because, they were hungry, or because they had food but they had no place to cook it. And we were getting transients, people from the bus station."

Quinlan, who now leads a Catholic church in Poquoson, said he tries, wherever he is assigned, to start a project that serves the neighborhood. On the Peninsula, it is a thrift store where unemployed watermen and their families can shop.

"In each area, we try to find out the real needs of real people, then answer them," he said.

The real need for hot, nutritious meals is met at St. Mary's with meat, vegetables, bread and sometimes dessert. The kitchen serves soup, but usually lunch is more substantial.

The menu depends on the generosity of other Catholic churches, Protestant churches, the Navy and agencies such as the Foodbank of Southeastern Virginia and SHARE. Susie Daniel, the kitchen's 73-year-old supervisor, prepares enough food to serve about 100 people. If she suspects she might run out, she goes to the church's pantry and pulls out enough canned goods to supplement the meal.

"Oh, I have some people who say, 'I don't like this. Give me something else,' but I tell them, I can't afford it. If you want something else, you'll have to go get it," Daniel said.

"Sometimes it's frustrating, but then we have good times, too, when I see these people come off the street, eat and enjoy it. Somebody usually comes by and tells me they thought it was good food," Daniel said.

Daniel, a former nurse's aide and babysitter who has been working since she was 12, became kitchen supervisor in March. She and one full-time helper prepare all the food. Parishioners from the church volunteer to set tables, serve and clean up after lunch.

Kirby Spratley, 33, ate at the soup kitchen for several months and asked repeatedly if he could work there. In January, he was hired as a helper.

Spratley said he knows what it's like to be homeless. He spent two years on the street and "still has one foot on the street and one foot in the door." He's trying to get his life together, keep a job, get off the street completely. He sometimes stays with his father or checks into the Union Mission.

"I was on the street, but I was never hungry," Spratley said. He ate often at St. Mary's and other area soup kitchens. But not everyone knows about free breakfasts, lunches and suppers served by churches and agencies such as the Salvation Army and the Union Mission.

"The soup kitchens help keep crime down," he said. "There's a lot of stealing when people are hungry. They'll do anything to eat."

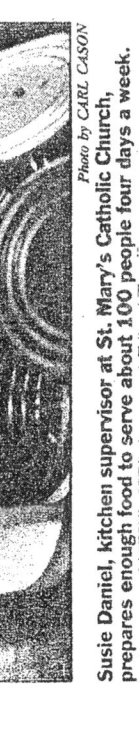

Photo by CARL CASON

Susie Daniel, kitchen supervisor at St. Mary's Catholic Church, prepares enough food to serve about 100 people four days a week.

Tidewater Living

The Virginian-Pilot THE LEDGER-STAR

SUNDAY DECEMBER 18, 1988

MEN & WOMEN/J4
DEAR ABBY, ANN LANDERS/J8

PART GRINCH,

PART GOOD

SHEPHERD,

FATHER TOM

QUINLAN

CONTINUES

TO ROCK

HIS FLOCK

Instead of saying, "You really all are biblical morons," the newly mellow T.Q. would say, "I can't believe where you're at."

Staff photos by LUI KIT WONG

GOING HIS WAY?

Quinlan currently says one weekend Mass in a Baptist church and another in a high-school cafeteria, but is raising money to build a church in these woods in Tabb.

By Bill Ruehlmann
Staff writer

A STARTLED MEMBER of the "Donahue" studio audience stared at the priest.

"If you don't believe in the Garden of Eden," she gasped, "how can you be a father?"

The Rev. Thomas J. Quinlan stared right back.

"I ain't no father," he snapped. "I gave it up."

Never address the controversial pastor of St. Kateri Tekawitha Catholic Church of Poquoson and Tabb as "Father Tom." Quinlan prefers "T.Q." This particular holiday season, he might willingly respond to at least one other name: Scrooge.

"I really believe in my heart," he rasps through a cloud of cigarette smoke at the Peninsula parish house, "that the Pope should get rid of Christmas. We didn't have it for the first 400 years. We invented it for good theological reasons, right? Now we can get rid of it and invent another feast day.

"I can't stand Christmas," he says. "It is the mother of American consumerism, sentimentality and depression. The Pope could get rid of it, but he won't. He wants to have his Polish baby Jesus."

Quinlan at 56 is no stranger to unpopular ecclesiastical opinion. He has, in the three stormy decades since his ordination, headed up Virginia congregations large and small,

"I really believe in my heart," says the Rev. Thomas J. Quinlan, "that the Pope should get rid of Christmas."

rich and poor, black and white. The constant has been outrage.

In him and at him.

"After American consumerism took over celebrating the Feast of the Incarnation," he complains, "it got to be the birthday of Jesus, and we weren't able to get to the main point, which is that God has erupted into human history. This is the moment we celebrate. But it's grown, and it's lost its meaning, and now they say it's a family day, a children's day. Then have another family day, children's day.

"As a church we're all called to baptize what's good, right?" he says. "We get into the real flesh world; we bless manure spreaders on the Feast of St. Isadore in Iowa. Equally, we're called to read the signs of the times and discern what is evil.

"To me, Christmas is bad, bad, bad. Ditch it."

Please see QUINLAN, Page J2

QUINLAN

continued from Page J1

The Grinch

On his day off, he looks beat.

Sprawled in a Poquoson living room, Quinlan does not present the avuncular appearance of breezy Bing Crosby in "Going My Way." He wears a worn purple sweater, no shirt; shapeless slacks scattered with cigarette ash; and loafers, no socks. One pair of spectacles clings precariously to the end of his nose; the other hangs from a chain around his neck. Bag-eyed, lean and balding, with haylike hair sticking straight out from his head, the loose-limbed priest resembles a blasted and aging Stan Laurel.

Or, more than a little, Dr. Seuss' elongated Grinch, whom Quinlan portrayed with real theatrical relish in last year's children's Christmas liturgy.

"Maybe Christmas," he thought, "doesn't come from a store. Maybe Christmas . . . perhaps . . . means a little bit more!"

This is not his house, though he resides here, in one bedroom. The rest belongs to the parishioners, who come and go at will. Over the mantle is a color photograph of the priest baptizing his nephew in a foamy Atlantic surf. In the kitchen, he keeps a Xerox machine.

The salient furnishing is books. Piles of them, walls of them. One shelf in his study contains volumes of memorabilia, including every critical letter he has ever received.

You permitted the Mass to be celebrated with vessels not lined with gold or silver, as required.

I intend to circulate a petition to the bishop for your recall as our pastor.

Your homilies churn my gastric juices!

Quinlan lights up another Cambridge 100 and takes one more swallow of black coffee.

"It was interesting on Donahue's show," he growls in his smoke-lacerated bass. "Twenty-two percent of the people said that Hitler would be in hell. Well, we don't know that.

"In the Catholic teaching, anybody can repent at the last moment. When I walk into heaven, I may see Hitler sitting on the bench. And 55 popes parked in hell, which is where Dante puts a lot of them."

He does not know how he was selected to appear on a panel debating the existence of an afterlife on Phil Donahue's program Oct. 24. But there he was, in the company of a fundamentalist, a universalist, an atheist and an advocate of reincarnation. And a studio audience of the usual intensity.

"It was," Quinlan says, "a zoo."

He enjoyed himself immensely. On the air, the priest argued that there was no Garden of Eden. Pandemonium.

"It's part of the Genesis myth," Quinlan says. "The author was faced with the human condition, the physical and spiritual parts of man, and there's something that pushes us toward good and evil, right? The Garden of Eden was just made up with the best theory to explain it.

"I mean, people with a minimal education know that a snake didn't come up and say, 'Hi, what're ya doin' there, lady?' And the lady said, 'I'd like to eat that banana.' We know it wasn't an apple, because we didn't have apples in those days.

"Or an avocado. Whatever the hell it was. Mango. I mean, just use your common sense.

"When you study it biblically, of course, then you really start on the Jewish-Christian pilgrimage of where reality is at, where he's at, what's the purpose, and it all comes to one big crescendo when God finally sent Jesus. Without that, I think the whole thing is nonsense."

Quinlan got calls, letters.

"The media picked up on the superficial side. But I expected that, just as I knew on the Donahue *show* it was going to run all over. It got hysterical, because the lady says, 'Is this person really a priest?'

"Well, the secretary of my first assignment of 30 years ago wrote to me from Alexandria, *and* she said, 'It sounded just like the people talking about you when you had been at Blessed Sacrament six months.' Nothing's changed."

Advent

Has the man mellowed?

"A little," he says. "Instead of saying, 'You really all are biblical morons,' which I said on many a Sunday at Good Shepherd, I say, 'I can't believe where you're at.' I'm beginning to appreciate how they got there — my senile state. But still, the same push and drive."

Quinlan took over Good Shepherd Church of Alexandria in 1971. Within three years, that once-staid, middle-class institution and its freewheeling pastor had made Time magazine. Time said: "At Good Shepherd, he derided the complacent laity as 'spiritual white trash' who merely dropped by the church to fill up at God's 'gas pump.' "

Quinlan walked up the aisle one Christmas as a bespangled Blue Angel, lampooning the secular holiday spirit; on Palm Sunday, he rode a forklift into the sacristy.

That wasn't the first time Quinlan rocked a flock, nor would it be the last.

"Sometimes," the priest says, "they view me as *coming from Mars*. But remember: I came from a blue-collar New England family. I had the same cultural and educational background as they: I had the Five First Saturdays and the Nine First Fridays and the rosary and all the stuff."

He was born in Springfield, Mass., the oldest of 10 children. He moved to Chicopee at 8 and attended public schools.

Upon graduation in 1948, he enrolled at Christ the King Seminary of St. Bonaventure in Orlean, N.Y., leaving twice before completing his studies to work for New York Central Railroad and a sporting goods store. Quinlan was ordained in Richmond in 1958 and assigned to Blessed Sacrament Catholic Church in Alexandria, where he remained five years. He then came to Sacred Heart in Norfolk.

1964: The newspaper clipping shows a crisply oiled and clipped Quinlan noting: "It *is necessary for a priest to leave no areas in* doubt when discussing matters of religion, morals and ethics." Straight enough.

By 1974, reporters are calling him "the hip-talking, long-haired new pastor" of St. Mary's in Norfolk, and he is responding, "So somebody says I'm a nut. If I know I'm not a nut, I don't care about it. You can't let people deter you if you know you're right."

In between were stints at Sacred Heart in Covington, St. Vincent de Paul in Newport News and the nationally noted Good Shepherd in Alexandria, where Quinlan permitted women to distribute communion.

What happened to T.Q.?

"The human tour of life," says the priest.

Built in 1791, St. Mary's, the oldest Catholic church in the state, had a 90 percent black, inner-city congregation. Quinlan remained its pastor for 11 volatile years.

"I'm trying to speak to the people where they're at," he said, and stood before his congregation in a Superman suit one Holy Week to burlesque false messiahs.

Norfolk welfare fraud investigator Barbara Wright remains a St. Mary's parishioner and close friend to Quinlan.

"Most people can't get beyond the facade he has of being a very abrupt person, a person who likes to shock people," she says. "I think he uses that technique to get people's attention. If you get beyond that, you'll find he's pretty much a traditional Catholic.

"If you can get beyond his flamboyant appearance to what he does and stands for, you'd have to like him," she says.

In recent years, there has been the matter of the priest's difficulty with the bottle.

"It was noted, especially by people who worked closely with him in the parish," Wright admits. "We knew it. Sometimes it did interfere.

"Catholics no longer put their priests on a pedestal, but some could not accept the drinking, and it probably turned them off," she says. "It did have an effect."

Dressed as Superman, Quinlan burlesqued false messiahs in a single bound at St. Mary's in Norfolk in 1979.

In 1964: Crisply oiled and clipped.

Offices

It affected the Rev. Thomas J. Quinlan most of all.

"I'm a romanticist," he says. "My Myers-Briggs (personality indicator) shows I'm excessively futuristically oriented. So I was in a black parish, and I needed a lot of support, and I felt I wasn't getting it, and I just got more and more — deromanticized.

"I consider it a vast male menopause," he says. "Even if it hadn't been drinking, it could have been something else. But I had to get from the romantic love of the church to the real pragmatic Vatican machine that I have to live with or leave."

He hurt. Human hypocrisy: backbiting, jealousy, dishonesty. Is this how real people are?

T.Q. looked into the bottom of his glass and saw a reflection.

"I went to one of those treatment programs, but it didn't help much," Quinlan says. "St. Luke's (Institute) in Maryland, which is terrible, a facility for clergy and nuns. That was Oct. 12, 1982; it was the bishop's idea."

Bishop Walter F. Sullivan of the Richmond diocese, a longstanding supporter of the priest, acknowledges his concern.

"Father Quinlan is a problem drinker," Sullivan says. "It was brought to my attention that the drinking had interfered with his priestly ministry, and I felt the necessity to intervene for his benefit and that of the parish. He has had a struggle with alcohol, he has had some relapses, but he has addressed the issue and confronted himself on it."

Not without difficulty.

"St. Luke's was a fundamentalistic program, no real integration of the spiritual and psychological," Quinlan says. "And, of course, I can't stand A(lcoholics) A(nonymous). To me, you go to an AA meeting, and it's like going to Rock Church. I never bought it."

But Quinlan stopped drinking?

"Yeah."

What did it?

"The conviction that either I was going to spend my time running away from reality by drinking or I was going to face reality, which is the church and where people are at. I faced institutional attitudes, like if 60 percent of priests leave the priesthood, then we will still have male, celibate priests."

He wrestles on with God. And with the church. When the priest left St. Mary's in 1985, it was not to go to another parish.

"I got mad at the bishop and floated," Quinlan says.

"He kind of needed some time away," Sullivan says. "He was exhausted. It was just a time to retool."

Meanwhile, the church became aware of demographic studies of York County that showed the population doubling in size.

"The bishop asked me, 'Wouldn't you like to start a new parish before you die?' " Quinlan says. "And I said, 'Yes, I'll try it.' We began May 28, 1986."

Downtown Poquoson is a wide place on Wythe Creek Road north of Hampton with a single traffic light. But that wide place extends to five lanes; with shopping centers on either side. A measure of the collision between past and future here resides in the names of two local realties: Bull Island, a title harking back to the region's fishing village beginnings; and Enterprise, an expression of its continuing suburban explosion beside Langley Air Force Base and NASA Langley Research Center.

Space-age St. Kateri Tekawitha parish is named for a native American.

"This was once a community of watermen and little farmers," Quinlan says. "When I came, I found a whole new pile of nouveau riche move-ins. The Episcopal church had started six months before, and the Presbyterians were getting ready to begin three months after."

Sociological evidence for an era: six pizzerias in Poquoson.

"Two working parents," the priest says. "They don't have time to cook. And pizza is expensive."

His predominantly white collar parish can afford it. But can the parish afford Quinlan?

"He has been very well received," reports church member Raymond Vernall, superintendent of Poquoson schools. "You don't have to be around T.Q. very long, particularly in a formal setting, to recognize his intense devotion to helping people. He does say things sometimes, and people will say, 'I don't believe he said that!' But he did.

"It almost leads them to say, 'Well, I guess I better come back to see what he's going to say next.' "

Mourning and morning

How about this: "The Vatican's worse than the Wizard of Oz for giving quick answers."

Or this: "Fundamentalists are the Shiite Moslems of America."

Or this: "In New York, so many of the parishes are Roman Catholic McDonald's. You go in and get your communion, your little host instead of bread, your spiritual food or symbol of unity or whatever you want to call it, and you go home. It's automated."

Parish associate Sue Wilkinson, a former religion teacher at Norfolk Catholic who has long known Quinlan, says, "T.Q. shoots from the hip. He's going to call it like it is. I think a lot of people here wanted a nice quiet little church that they could come to on Sunday and go home and say, 'Oh yes, we went to church.' As he would phrase it, 'the sacramental fast-food people.'

"And he has not allowed people to do that," she says. "He has really challenged the community to be involved. The challenge to this parish is: 'Every family a 5 percent tither, every adult member a minister.' If you're not growing, you're not listening to T.Q."

To date, 152 families, 500 people, are listening, Saturdays at Yorkminster Baptist Church in Tabb and Sundays in Poquoson High School auditorium. Tithes for the second Sunday in Advent amounted to $2,662.20. On the back of the church bulletin, a notation: *90 pledges have come in averaging $25.76 per week (low for our parish!). Would the other 62 please hand them in today?*

And another: *Our Thrift Shop is moving to the Poquoson Shopping Center. This is our Parish Community Project. We ask all to come today at 1 p.m. with station wagons and trucks to help us move. This is no small undertaking, since our Parish only opened the original Thrift Shop a year ago.*

It is a witness to you people's sense of service to the poor, and there are plenty of them in Poquoson and Tabb!

One can surmise the source for these exclamations.

"It's gonna cost us, God knows, several million dollars to put up our church building," Quinlan rasps. "But we weren't here a year and set up the thrift shop, because the watermen and the natives will not ask for help. They won't even go on welfare, a lot of them, because of self-pride.

"The church has two groups: one that says we can't afford to deal with them, and the other that says there are no poor in Poquoson.

"So one of my tasks is to convince these people, if we're Christians, that the poor is one of our first concerns. Nothing to do with Thanksgiving, in the last few weeks York-Poquoson social services have been calling me, and I have had to bring food to people who don't have any, even to these apartments here."

He gestures out the picture window toward tight new clusters of suburban townhouses.

"So there are a lot of needy people, if you don't want to call them poor, all over the place," he says.

This is the belief that will not leave Quinlan alone. Nor will he leave the belief alone. In agony and celebration.

"What's good about Catholicism?"

One of the church's most consistent critics stabs out a Cambridge 100 and answers his own rhetorical question.

"Its universality. Its blessing of every kind of culture conceivable, like the Pope going to the Papuans, to the Indians at the Arctic Circle. When it is faithful to its traditions, the church believes and works on the absolute coequality of all men and women."

The cross and the totem pole.

This fall, T.Q. was wakened in the parish house at 3 a.m. A parishioner had died. He dressed quickly and left to be with the family until dawn.

Then he drove home, changed clothes, and the Rev. Thomas J. Quinlan departed again to say Sunday Mass.

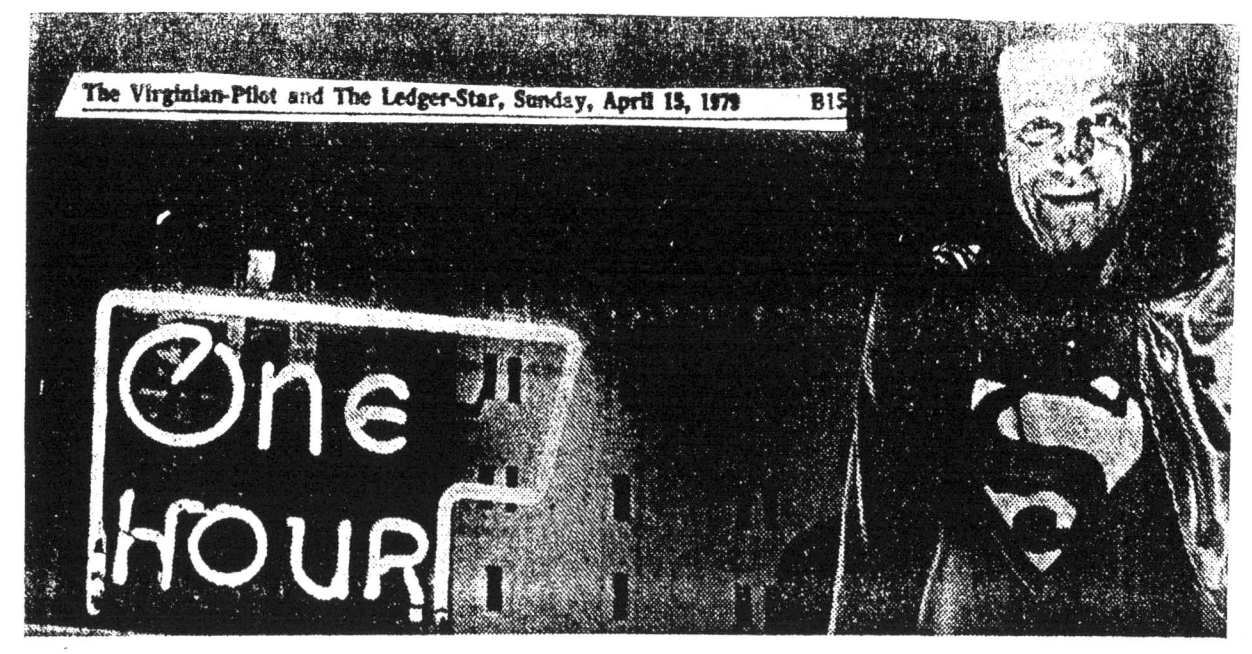

The Virginian-Pilot and The Ledger-Star, Sunday, April 15, 1979 B15

Quinlan as Superman hovers over "Metropolis," a set made of cardboard boxes and neon signs.

St. Mary's Mighty Superman Brought to His Knees by Jesus

By STACEY BURLING
Virginian-Pilot Staff Writer

NORFOLK—It's a bird. It's a plane. It's Superman. No. It's the Rev. Tom Quinlan, up to his old tricks. Last year it was Star Wars. Before that, the Wiz.

Now, the priest of St. Mary's Catholic Church, clad in a red and blue Superman suit, is standing amid a cardboard and neon Metropolis. The set hides the 22-ton marble altar in the state's oldest Catholic church.

It's all part of services at the church and Quinlan's way of saying that Jesus is the real Superman in language he thinks people today will understand.

"It's as old as the human race," the tall, thin, white priest of a 95 percent black parish said. "It's always been that people want a superman. People are always looking for a messiah other than Jesus."

They miss the Gospel's message that "you've got to drink in what's been done already," he said. Istead of looking to Jesus, "they run after all kinds of superprophets and faith healers."

At 47, the chain-smoking Quinlan looks a lot more like Bob Hope than Superman. His lined face is framed by shaggy hair and his deep voice has a ragged quality.

He swears he doesn't like the part and begs to be released from his bright blue tights and red satin cape. He looks more at home in the horn-rimmed glasses that mark his other role in the Superman story as Clark Kent, reporter for the Rising Son.

"I usually help write these scripts so other people can do it," he said.

The script, written by two members of the liturgy committee, is supposed to parallel the Gospel according to Mark.

The apostles wanted a Superman, just like all their descendants, Quinlan said.

"They didn't want a messiah who said you got to suffer and die and all that."

In the church version of the classic comic, which began on Ash Wednesday, Feb. 28, Superman ultimately is defeated by a black paperboy, the Jesus figure.

Superman stands helpless while villain Lex Luthor taunts him with a piece of kryptonite. Jesus shows he's stronger than Superman by lifting a cross. "That's the end of Superman," Quinlan says with obvious delight.

The plot ended Saturday night, in time for Easter, with a "Eucharistic Brunch with the Futuristic Crunch." In that scene, Clark Kent, Lois Lane, and the rest of the cast reflect on Superman's demise while they drink bloody mary's and eat eggs.

Quinlan hopes the play will make the Bible, written 1,900 years ago, more real to modern people.

"It says the same thing," he said. "You've got to get the message across and most people ain't Bible scholars. It's been very effective, I think."

While members of a church in Alexandria Quinlan copastored balked at his unorthodox ways, membership at St. Mary's has more than tripled during his 4½-year reign.

Quinlan thinks his largely black congregation is more receptive to symbols and better able to interpret them than previous groups he's directed.

Never one to revere tradition, Quinlan raised more than a few eyebrows when he drove a white Volkswagen into church to prove Jesus would have used a "humble" vehicle. His parishioners dressed as toys one Christmas. He was the Blue Angel.

If nothing else, he may have gained a certain acceptance even from opponents like Robert Forrest, a member of the Roman Catholic Confraternity. That group is campaigning for a return of traditional masses.

"Nothing he would do would surprise me," Forrest said with a chuckle. "There are certain things in life, you just ignore and keep going the other way."

As for Quinlan, he hasn't outdone himself yet.

"I've got a thousand more ideas," he said. "But I won't tell them."

Community church built to house spirit

By Alayna DeMartini
Post News Editor

Reverend Thomas J. Quinlan's words of caution to the architect that will build Poquoson's first Catholic church were "If you build it like a church, I'll sue you."

Quinlan pastor of the Saint Kateri Tekakwitha Church, does not want to build a traditional Catholic church on the 14 acre wooded property on Big Bethel Road, he says.

Instead of stained glass windows, Quinlan wants the church to have several spacious windows that overlook the 100 foot trees in the surrounding woods.

Video cameras took the place of stain glass windows, Quinlan says. "They're still life movies, that were lovely in the 12th century," but now they're outdated.

A steeple or marble are definitely out of the question, he adds.

Not all the benches for the congregants will face the altar he says, which is the traditional church design. They will instead face the altar from different angles.

Architectural plans for the building are rolled up in a cardboard box in Quinlan's Wythe Creek Road office. They are the product of three years of discussion about the future church.

Quinlan and members of the church's building committee are the first to admit that planning the church has been a slow and bureaucratic process.

Building committee members have had to present their plan to the York County board of Supervisors and the county's planning board, twice. The Board of Supervisors recently granted the church a waiver to build a 50 foot cathedral ceiling although the area is zoned with a 35 foot limit.

They have also had to consult with the Army Corps. of Engineers for permission to build on the five acres that are not designated wetlands.

Despite the bureaucracy, building committee member Sally Neher is enthusiastic.

"Churches cannot be built overnight," Neher says. "It took 600 years to build the first temple."

St. Kateri Tekawitha Church, which was founded four years ago, has been meeting on Saturday evenings at Christ the Episcopal Church down the street from the future site on Big Bethel Road.

The Sunday service is in the Poquoson High School auditorium which seats about 300 people. On Christmas and Easter, the auditorium is often standing room only.

The church will be the third on Big Bethel Road, but it will be the first to include three other buildings under the same roof.

In addition to the church that will seat 800 people, plans for the $4 million Catholic Community center include three other buildings which will be used for social gatherings and religious education.

The first building to be erected will be the social hall which will be used for club meetings, funeral dinners and wedding receptions, Quinlan says.

It will house the Saturday and Sunday services until the church sanctuary is built.

The "Commons" will be the second and smaller social hall for gathering before and after services, Quinlan says.

The building which will be constructed third is the education and administration building which will house the religious education classes and the church offices.

The church sanctuary will be constructed last because it is the most costly and it can be used only for services and concerts, Quinlan says.

The site will also include approximately 9 acres of area that will not be built on and can be used for a nature walk.

"It's good for the neighbors to have a place. As the city gets crowded there are fewer places to go for walks," he says.

One woman already has plans to use it as a jogging trail, Quinlan remarks.

"You won't know that a church is there except for the sign," he says, explaining that it will be set back 200 feet from the road.

Although the church building will be new to the community, the church has existed for several years, says Quinlan, who is adament that a building is not necessary to have a church.

"There were no church buildings for the first three hundred years of the Catholic religion," Quinlan says. "They (catholics) met in other people's homes."

The new community center will bring the members some identity, and most likely it will attract more members, Quinlan says.

"People were interested for the identity," he says. "From the beginning, they pledged they were committed to that."

Please see **Church**, page 12

Before the church was started, Catholics had to go as far as Hampton or Yorktown to attend services, Quinlan says.

Some Catholics in the area don't like meeting in other buildings, observes Tom Reid, who is a charter member of the church. Instead they travel as far as Hampton to attend Catholic services at Bethel Manor or Langley Air Force Base, he says.

Although Sally Neher has never minded attending Sunday services in the Poquoson High School auditorium, she anticipates that the new church will draw the community together.

"It will be a focal point for the community," Neher says. "... a means of drawing the community together."

When she first moved to Poquoson, Neher said she worried that there wasn't a central community church, despite the tight knit group of Catholic families in Poquoson and Tabb.

FREE   SERVING THE PENINSULA   VOLUME 1, NUMBER 11

Quinlan's unorthodox methods have brought him unwanted attention from Rome

Priest puts twist on traditional dogma

Ecology a focus at Poquoson parish

by Marjorie Mayfield
Special to Senior Times

Father Tom Quinlan, 59, is Irish, and he is a Roman Catholic priest. But that's where the similarities to Bing Crosby's character in the film *The Bells of St. Mary's* end.

Fr. Quinlan made Time magazine the time he celebrated Christmas Mass dressed as "the blue angel." That was in the early 1970s, when the Catholic church was experimenting with worship for the first time in centuries, and Quinlan was in the vanguard. A few years later, also in a Northern Virginia parish, Fr. Quinlan drove down the aisle in an orange Volkswagen while children threw confetti. In both cases, 2,000-year-old Biblical teachings needed re-interpreting with modern symbols, he believed. His suburban parishioners might not catch the humility of Jesus riding into town on a donkey instead of an Arabian stallion on Palm Sunday.

But they could understand Fr. Quinlan's orange VW compared to their own Cadillacs and Mercedes parked outside. "We're not a bunch of Jews or Arabs running around in the first century, you know?" Fr. Quinlan explains.

Please see Priest 10

Fr. Quinlan's congregation has grown to over 500 families.

Priest
Continued from page 1

in the Catholic Diocese of Richmond, brilliant, bold, irascible, Fr. Quinlan is still at it, though five years ago his avant-guard tactics helped land him in near-exile, a rural Peninsula assignment where his fledgling congregation did not even have a building.

At Poquoson High School, where the congregation of St. Kateri Tekakwitha meets, the auditorium was packed and wild with excitement two Christmases ago as Fr. Quinlan in a train conductor's uniform punched tickets. He was dramatizing the book, "Polar Express," during the children's liturgy.

The congregation spent a recent Lent worshipping around a cardboard Berlin Wall built of hundreds of milk cartons. Members scribbled their sins as graffiti on the wall, then burned it when Easter arrived.

A fledgling congregation no more, the parish of 560, named for a Native American saint, expects to move shortly into a $900,000 church, the first phase of a building project.

Fr. Quinlan's dramatics, as well as his forthright questioning of many Catholic moral teachings, are "a shock" that has "turned off as many as it turned on," says one parish leader, Tom Andres. Yet Mr. Andres and other parishioners say they have come to value Fr. Quinlan's as a scholarly, inquiring mind, bent on forcing people to think for themselves.

Mr. Andres, a retired Naval commander, says he grew up in conservative Catholic parishes in the North. "There it's 'Gerber' religion," Andres says, referring to the baby food. "Pablum. Somebody chews it up for you and spits it up and all you have to do is swallow it."

Fr. Quinlan, on the other hand, "is saying, 'Hey - You've got to have a mature religion. You've got to stand on your own two feet and make decisions." Mr. Andres says he used to forget a service as soon as he left church. With Fr. Quinlan, "I'll find myself on a Wednesday saying, 'Who does that so-and-so think he is, saying things like that?"

Modern science is rapidly antiquating many moral teachings of the Catholic church, Fr. Quinlan says. For instance, the church teaches that homosexual acts are sinful. Fr. Quinlan believes that pronouncement should at least be re-studied in the light of modern understandings. "There are new scientific discoveries for the basis of homosexuality. The Vatican calls it a disorder. Well, they just come to that conclusion too quickly; they haven't even investigated it," he says.

The same goes for "contraception and the whole bag" of sexual issues, "even abortion, which too many priests make their one moral issue," Fr. Quinlan continues. "How can they be so certain that at the moment the sperm fertilizes the egg, that's a human being? I think they have to re-think it ..."

Fr. Quinlan keeps his congregation after Mass to explore such matters through study of a recent book, "Catholic Morality Revisited," by Gerard S. Sloyan. At least 100 people usually stay for the Sunday discussions.

Francie O'Donohue, 57, is one who appreciated Fr. Quinlan's frankness and his willingness to face difficult issues from the moment he arrived in Poquoson. "I thought, boy, I've been waiting for this all my life. I needed TRUTH."

She described Fr. Quinlan's teaching style as "very down-to-earth, a very real approach to what life is all about. Who needs fairy tales? Life is too harsh."

Five years ago, Ms O'Donohue learned just how harsh life can be when she lost her son. One phone call and Fr. Quinlan was there, after midnight, to be with she and her husband until they left for a plane. "Yes, he is outspoken," Ms O'Donohue says. "But there is the other side that is the best friend you would ever have in the whole world."

As evidence of the pastor's compassion, Ms O'Donohue points to Fr. Quinlan's starting Poquoson's only thrift shop for the poor as well as the town's central food pantry, the latter operated out of Fr. Quinlan's office.

Poquoson is home to many struggling watermen. But almost all his parishioners are professionals and "move-ins," many of them scientists working with local offices of the National Aeronautics and Space Administration.

At Kateri Tekakwitha, Fr. Quinlan is pushing the cutting-edge on more yuppie terms, focusing on ecology as a moral imperative and experimenting with the latest Catholic reform, breaking large anonymous parishes into small communities, not unlike Baptist Sunday Schools, for study and faith-sharing.

Even the congregation's new sanctuary will be avant-guard, erected largely of glass and looking onto 14 acres of dense woods that the parish does not plan to clear. Most churches have no trees around them, a feature the ecology-minded Poquoson parish could not understand. Says Fr. Quinlan: "I told the architect, if you make it look like a church, I'll sue you."

Ministries building dedicated

Bishop Walter F. Sullivan recently blessed the St. Kateri Tekakwitha Ministries Building in Poquoson which contains a thrift shop, central food pantry, chapel and parish offices. Father Thomas J. Quinlan, pastor of the parish, led the procession. Others who followed with Bishop Sullivan were Rev. Isabel Steilberg, of Christ the King Episcopal Church, Tabb, and Father Roy P. White, pastor of Trinity United Methodist, Poquoson.

Ex-Ben Franklin store houses thrift shop, Mass

Tabb church acts despite red tape

By Cindy Cusic Micco
Special to The Catholic Virginian

St. Kateri Tekakwitha parish has been like the man without a country — it is a church without a building. Now that has changed, but not exactly according to plan.

Since its founding in 1986, the parish that is named for the first American Indian proposed for sainthood has been planning and praying to build on a heavily wooded 14-acre tract in York County's Tabb community near Poquoson.

The tract has come under considerable governmental regulation, however, because it is considered wetlands, said Father Thomas J. Quinlan, pastor of St. Kateri Tekakwitha.

It is taking years for governmental agencies to give the go-ahead for St. Kateri Tekakwitha to proceed with its four-phase plan of construction that will include an 800-seat hall, a worship space, a commons area and a Christian education building, he said.

The parish celebrates Sunday Mass now at Poquoson High School and, until recently, held its Saturday evening services at a nearby Episcopal church.

Now the Saturday services are held at a 16,200-square-foot building in downtown Poquoson that the parish bought for its social outreach ministries with a $300,000 loan from Bishop Walter F. Sullivan, said Father Quinlan.

"We got this building before we got our temple," he quipped as he gave a tour of the spacious building that used to be a Ben Franklin store.

The Parish Thrift Shop, which raised $13,000 to help the poor last year, already fills half the downstairs space in the two-story building. The building also houses the Central Food Pantry for Poquoson and Tabb, which is supported by two Methodist churches along with St. Kateri Tekakwitha. (Although the parish's patron, Kateri Tekakwitha, the Lily of the Mohawks, has not yet been declared a saint by Rome, the Tabb Catholic community has anticipated her canonization. As Father Quinlan explains, the parish is "following centuries of tradition" in which saints were declared by the local people.)

For now, the parish offices and a small chapel area for Saturday evening services fill out the downstairs of the building. Once the church building is completed in Tabb and the offices move there, Father Quinlan envisions turning that space into a Youth Center for middle school kids.

"They're the ones who get in a lot of trouble — sixth, seventh and eight graders," he said. The children come home from school to an empty house "and they're bored."

The youth center will include a large meeting room, a video game room and a study area, said Father Quinlan. The parish's justice and peace committee is working on the details of how the youth center will operate, he added.

As for the unfinished upstairs of the building, Father Quinlan said he envisions turning that into subsidized apartments for the elderly. The location seems ideal, he said, because it is within walking distance of shopping, banks and doctors' offices.

Buying a $300,000 outreach building has made some parishioners uneasy, said Father Quinlan, because they fear they won't get their church building in Tabb. But the thrift shop is self sufficient with its own checkbook that is separate from the church's finances, he said.

One of the exciting things about having the outreach building is that it gives the parish a presence in Poquoson that will not be lost when the church is built in Tabb, said Father Quinlan.

St. Kateri Tekakwitha Church's new outreach building is located in the heart of Poquoson.

Father Thomas J. Quinlan stands with Parish Thrift Shop volunteers Fra O'Donohue, left, and Zeola Fox, who are members of St. Kateri Tekakwith parish.

The new church will be located in a highly residential area that is not convenient for people in need to visit, he continued.

"There are plenty of poor people here, he said. Many are too proud to take cha ity, but they will wander into the Paris Thrift Shop and pay for items, he said.

Church answers needs

By Alayna DeMartini
Post News Editor

Thomas Quinlan has heard many legends in his day, including the one he heard five years ago about there being no poor people in Poquoson.

But Quinlan, who became the first pastor of the Catholic Church St. Kateri Tekakwitha started a year round food bank because he didn't believe what he had heard.

His experience over the last five years has justified his original skepticism.

Although the median household income of $47,345 is higher than that of the rest of the Peninsula, some city residents face the monthly threat of ... ing their utilities ... on for not paying a bill.

Others face eviction from their homes for being unable to pay their rent or are plagued with delinquent doctor bills or car payments.

Help for those stru'gl' with finances is often abundant d— the holidays whe— ... ous, Poquoson chur— ... and civic organizatio— ... clothing, food a— ... generously in the spirit of the season.

But for the remainder of the year, where can residents in need turn?

Saint Kateri Tekakwitha Church is one resource for those in need in Poquoson throughout the year and this year the number of people seeking food or help with finances has dramatically increased, Quinlan said.

Food is donated by members of St. Kateri Tekakwitha, Tabernacle United Methodist and Christ the King Episcopal churches.

The food supply has dwindled to a few sparsely filled shelves and freezer items. A package of calf livers, a box of peas and carrots and a few bags of green vegetables and rolls are the few frozen items left in the church's freezer.

"We've had less than this before," said Elaine Riley, who helps coordinate the food bank and makes home grocery deliveries. "The variety is good however," she said, explaining that a few different people could pick out a few weeks of groceries, she said.

Those same food shelves were packed after the holidays, said Quinlan, who is adamantly opposed to holiday food giving which he calls the "Christmas, Thanksgiving and Easter Syndrome."

"I think it is confusing," he said.

Along with food, a frequent request is for help in financing rent or utilities bills. The money for

Need
Continued from page 1

these payments comes from church collections and from profits from the Parish Thrift Shop on Wythe Creek Road.

The fund ran out last month, two weeks before the start of the new fiscal year O—

"— —see it —tting —
better," he said. "I have to think it is going to get worse."

People seeking the church's services help most often call the church and some are referred by neighbors, friends or social workers from the York-Poquoson Social Services office.

Some families in need are identified by school principals, Quinlan said, adding that last year families of 12 students received $50 food vouchers from their program.

Along with the vouchers, families can come to the office and pick out food or if they do not have transportation, Quinlan will deliver food.

Providing food can be a sensitive issue with the recipients, Quinlan said, adding that "many would starve before they would accept a basket."

For residents who chose to remain anonymous, Quinlan places the food basket on their doorstep quietly leaves.

The stigma associated with what some perceive to be "handouts," has discouraged some residents in need, Quinlan said.

Along with providing food, the church also provides inexpensive used clothing through the Parish Thrift store.

The clothing store also benefits the donors Quinlan said, by forcing them to get rid of their materialism.

"It's important to preserve the dignity of the poor and suddenly marginalized," Quinlan explained. Their goal is to help people "who fall in the cracks of the system," those are not poor enough to qualify for subsidized housing or food stamps but not wealthy enough to afford daily necessities themselves.

The most common request Quinlan receives is from female single parents whose husbands abandoned them suddenly with little notice or food, he said.

> "Many would rather starve than accept a basket."
> — Thomas Quinlan

One of those individuals was helped last week when she contacted the office requesting groceries, after her husband left her and her two sons with two days of food on their shelves. She called the church office to come by to pick.

When individuals call or come into the office seeking food or financial assistance, Riley said that before extending help they usually ask the individual who is helping them pay their bills. There are no qualifications for receiving the church's assistance, Riley said.

"It is very traumatic to have to come in for help," she said. "It's a tough thing to have to say."

The church is beginning a program to help finance dental bills.

One of the most neglected needs of the poor is dental care, Quinlan said because "it appears to be the least urgent need. . . A lot of people do something about their general health, but ignore their teeth."

After nine years as traveling church, St. Kateri Tekakwitha has a home

By Cindy Cusic Micco
Special to The Catholic Virginian

From the wetlands of York County has arisen a church of glass and concrete that will — at last — serve the parish of St. Kateri Tekakwitha.

The peaceful setting of the $1.2 million white structure in Tabb belies the aggravation its parish has been through to get it built. The task has taken nine years because its lovely wooded setting is classified "wetlands" and that means a string of governmental approval was needed before construction could begin.

But the wait is over and St. Kateri Tekakwitha was formally dedicated Wednesday, March 27.

"Your journey as a parish faith community has certainly been unique," Bishop Walter F. Sullivan said at the dedication liturgy. "Yours is the first parish to purchase a social action center for a thrift shop before building a place of worship. In a way both places are acts of honor and homage to God because you are reaching out as Jesus did in love of God to those in need here in Poquoson."

The bishop spoke of the parish's patron who was a native American woman born in an Indian village in a place now known as Auresville, N.Y., where there is a shrine to the North American martyrs.

"At the age of 20 Kateri was baptized a Catholic by one of the Jesuits and soon fled for her safety to the area of Montreal where she died four years later," Bishop Sullivan said. "It was in 1980 that Pope John Paul II beatified her because of her holiness of life. Your pastor has already canonized Kateri because he always keeps ahead of the church."

Until the March 27 dedication St. Kateri parishioners had a variety of homes.

"We've been a traveling church for 9 years," said Father Thomas J. Quinlan, pastor of St. Kateri. He noted they have used eight worship spaces, including an Episcopal church, a Baptist church and the local high school. The parish also has been through six thrift shops, five offices and three rectories.

It gained some stability in September 1994 when it bought a ministries building in downtown Poquoson and located its thrift shop and offices there along with a worship space for Saturday evening Masses.

In honor of its gypsy nature, Father Quinlan quipped, "We're all going to have beads and scarves for Palm Sunday for the parade" with neighboring parishes.

The church actually is a hall — the first of a four-phase plan that calls for a commons area, church, and education-administration building to be built in the future.

Spaciousness is the word that first comes to mind as you walk into the airy structure where the ceiling is 45 feet high at its peak. Walls of glass at either end, with a geometric pattern running through them, bring in light and the great outdoors.

When used as a hall, the building could accommodate 800 people at a sit-down dinner and up to 1,500 at other functions, explained Father Quinlan, who added he's already had calls from people interested in renting it.

Along the sides of the building are a commercial kitchen, storage room, classroom space, offices, a nursery, a cloak room and restrooms.

Exterior of St. Kateri Tekakwitha Church in Tabb.

Forty-five-foot high ceiling with glass walls bring light to interior.

From the worship space in the middle of the building, you can gaze out at the parish's 14 acres of land, nine of which is wooded. Father Quinlan said he plans to move the main altar around "whenever I feel like it." A small glass-enclosed room will be the minor worship area, he said.

Father Quinlan said it is especially important to him that the parish will have two presences in the community — the church in Tabb and the ministries building in Poquoson.

The parish patron is the first American Indian proposed for sainthood. Although the "Lily of the Mohawks" has not yet been declared a saint by Rome, the Tabb Catholic community has anticipated her canonization and followed "centuries of tradition" in which saints were declared by the local people, according to Father Quinlan.

40TH
ANNIVERSARY OF ORDINATION

AND

PRE-FUNERAL GALA

FOR

REV. THOMAS J. QUINLAN

ORDAINED
MAY 1, 1958

CELEBRATED THIS DAY
MAY 3, 1998

ST. KATERI TEKAKWITHA CATHOLIC CHURCH
3800 BIG BETHEL ROAD
TABB VIRGINIA

'TQ,' unusual man celebrates 40 years of priestly ministry

By Susan Bruno
Special to The Catholic Virginian

It's the proverbial match made in Heaven: Father Thomas J. Quinlan as pastor of St. Kateri Tekakwitha parish. Bishop Walter Sullivan assigned the remarkably unconventional priest to found the parish with undoubtedly the most unusual name in the Diocese of Richmond.

And because the match was so well crafted, the parish (whose name anticipates eventual sainthood for Blessed Kateri Tekakwitha, the Native American girl known as the Lily of the Mohawks) has grown steadily. By his own admission, so has its pastor, now 67, who's spent the last 12 years as leader in the mostly white, decidedly upscale Peninsula parish. When he arrived 11 years ago, there were 60 families; today it's 211. The growth, he admits, has been slow. "I make certain demands. I'm not running a McDonald's here. I'm not here to hand out Jesus-cookies."

These demands include a 5 percent tithe and active participation in at least one of the church's many religious and social ministries. "It's really minimal," said Father Quinlan — TQ, as he is called by nearly all. "But some just can't take the heat. They think I'm not watching, so they simply fade into the congregation. But I do notice. And I purge."

About every three months he challenges members who haven't gotten actively involved. "That's when they realize I'm serious. That's generally when they decide to look for another parish."

TQ doesn't take it personally. After all, taking heat for the unusual has been his legacy. This is the priest who once rode a tractor down the aisle of an inner-city church to rouse people's attention. He's the pastor who loaded a parish of black Catholics on a bus for a trip to the place where the slave Nat Turner was condemned to death. He once arranged to have 1,054 parishioners floated down the Potomac River on a ship to celebrate Easter Vigil. He also mounted a full-scale production of "The Wiz" in church one Lenten season – replete with 3,000 yellow bricks lining the main aisle of his church – with the congregation arriving in Emerald City on Easter.

Stunts? Hardly. They're intended to make a point about the liturgy being celebrated.

While many consider TQ a renegade priest, it's a moniker of which he is proud. His self-written epitaph is simple: He was odd. None who have met him are ambivalent – and his followers are legion. He has inspired thousands with his hard-hitting, unorthodox, "in your face" brand of Catholicism.

But it didn't start out that way, he admits. The eldest of 10 children in a fiercely Irish Catholic family in Springfield, Mass., he gravitated to the Richmond diocese and was ordained in Sacred Heart Cathedral on May 1, 1958. In search of a diocese that needed help, he checked out Manchester, N.H. and Trenton, N.J. But the fit wasn't right. "Then I heard they needed help in the Diocese of Richmond," he said. The rest, as they say, is history. He started out as a clean-cut, quiet, traditional priest. As he matured, he honed a personal style that more than once has made headlines.

Over the years, TQ has served in parishes all around the diocese: Blessed Sacrament, Alexandria; Keyser, W.Va.; Sacred Heart, Norfolk; Sacred Heart, Covington; Good Shepherd, Mount Vernon; St. Vincent's, Newport News; St. Mary's, Norfolk; and his current post, where he'd be just as happy to stay for the remainder of his active priestly ministry. "When you get to be my age, it is an option," he said, smiling.

His congregations have included the affluent, highly educated Pentagon types as well as the middle class and the desperately poverty stricken. He's led black parishes, mixed parishes, totally white parishes. And he's learned some basics as a result.

"Most Catholics are Biblical morons," he said. But that's just one of many challenges he has faced.

"There are some Catholics who simply don't like the post-Vatican II message. They want things the way they used to be. But that's never going to happen again. Some people just can't adapt to the new breath of Vatican II," he said. "When I was first ordained, it was a very clerical church. Since Vatican II, the people have become the church."

The church is ripe for Vatican III, he believes. "It's time to discuss things such as priests marrying, the ordination of women, and a redefinition of the Order of Deacons. It's time to talk about adaptation of the church to the modern world."

This isn't blasphemy coming from a man who, according to the Myers-Briggs Type Indicator personality test was found to be "excessively, futuristically oriented." It came as no surprise to TQ. Many people have told him he is a man born before his time. And it has borne itself out, he admits. "I'm not concerned with where the church is and has been," he said. "I'm more concerned with where it will be in the year 2005."

Someday priests will be allowed to marry, but he doubts women will ever be ordained. "It's not a gender issue," Quinlan said. "It's a matter of male power brokers in Rome not wanting to let go."

But things are going to have to change, he predicted. "We're in the post-immigrant era of the church. It used to be the spiritual center of everyone's lives, but that's no longer the case."

In many ways, Father Quinlan feels he has come full circle. As he celebrates his 40th anniversary of his ordination, he has found solace in a parish that allows him the latitude to practice his faith the way that he likes best. TQ's service to God is done today the way he has always done it: enthusiastically, flamboyantly and imbued with a lesson in humanity that, frankly, has on occasion found some parishioners looking elsewhere for spiritual guidance.

"Some people can't take the heat," he repeated one sunny afternoon, kicking back at a beach house on North Carolina's Outer Banks, a place he has escaped to for many years to relax, reflect and find escape from the pressures of pastoral responsibility. But relaxing TQ-style means voracious reading. He freely quotes the Bible, passages from great literature, Broadway shows and the secular press. He is obviously wise and, especially for those who go the extra mile to do God's work, caring. He has a wry sense of humor and a flair usually reserved for celebrities.

This radical priest is also a control freak. His 40th anniversary celebration, held May 3, was as unusual as you would expect. While toasting (and roasting) his history as a priest, he had guests help him celebrate his wake and funeral. (It included a New Orleans-style funeral procession, let by a combo playing "Just a Closer Walk With Thee," and empty white coffin in a hearse and the jubilarian seated in the front seat of a white funeral limousine.) In attendance, in addition to many past and present parishioners, were members of his family – lots of them. "I have 16 niece and nephews, and 26 grandnieces and grandnephews. Not bad when you consider my father was an only child," he beamed.

Msgr. Thomas Caroluzza, pastor of Holy Spirit in Virginia Beach and Episcopal Vical for Southeastern Virginia, recalled thoughts of his good friend, Father Quinlan: "Early on TQ was chided by his peers as being a heretic."

Msgr. Caroluzza and Father Quinlan met the night before their ordination to the priesthood. Both were assigned to parishes in Alexandria immediately thereafter, and they became life-long friends.

"While TQ's peers teased him for his unorthodox approach to ministering to his congregations, the bishop knew he was a good priest," Msgr. Caroluzza said. "There's always controversy surrounding TQ — but he always comes out smelling like a rose."

The most influential book in TQ's life was Feast of Fools by Harvard religious sociologist Harvey Cox, Msgr. Caroluzza said. Published in the late '60s, the book helped Father Quinlan "revive that medieval sense of fantasy and festivity. That's what he's all about," he said. "Imaginative fantasy strikes a chord in people's souls — and TQ taps into that."

"The 40th anniversary was a marvelous celebration," Bishop Sullivan told The Catholic Virginian. "In every assignment Father Quinlan has ever had, he's touched people very deeply because of the demands he makes upon them to be church in new ways.

"He has a loyal following throughout all of Virginia," Bishop Sullivan added, "and he has the deep respect of the priests."

In retrospect, his vocation has had its highs and lows. He's been able to use his love of theater in getting across the message of Jesus Christ. He's made many close friends. The regrets are few.

"Perhaps I might not have been so hard on my people," TQ said. "Everything was so clear to me. I couldn't understand why my parishioners didn't get it."

Had he not entered the priesthood what career path might he have chosen?

"Myers-Briggs said I would have been best suited to be an English teacher or an actor. But I would have better enjoyed playing accordion in a Polish orchestra or managing a 7-Eleven somewhere."

After his 40th anniversary Mass, whose principal celebrant and homilist was Bishop Walter F. Sullivan, Father Thomas J. Quinlan stood beside an open white coffin to greet his guests. He styled the jubilee celebration his 40th Anniversary of Ordination and Pre-Funeral Gala.

Readers write about vocations, TQ and Eucharist

■LETTERS From Page 6

About TQ

A friend gave us a copy of the May 18 issue of *The Catholic Virginian*. In reading the article about TQ we again knew why we have cancelled our subscription.

Is TQ in love with the church or his own style? Is he speaking on behalf of his Father or promoting his own agenda? Is TQ more interested in acting and entertaining or in feeding the Body of Christ? The clear mandate for every local shepherd (priest) is not to have "a loyal following throughout all of Virginia," but to lead his local flock in following the Great Shepherd.

The church isn't ready for Vatican III so long as we have priests and bishops who haven't understood the message of Vatican II: a bold call to holiness and renewal of all things in Christ through the church; a challenge to humility, true repentance, renewal of the inner life in Christ and a deep love and willing obedience to the teachings of the church. This is quite different from the TQ call: "Let's do it my way."

No, the decision not to ordain women is not about "power brokers in Rome not wanting to let go." Could it be that TQ, who so dislikes authority, wants to keep his personal authority by keeping the word "Catholic" while eroding in word and deed the very foundation of our precious life-giving faith?

And no, it is not "time to talk about adaptation of the church to the modern world." How foreign to the Gospel. The church is called to be the "light of the world." The real issue is to know what is light and what is dark and to flood the darkness with the ever-ancient and ever-new Light of the World.

Those who are enthralled by TQ are like children awe-struck by July 4th fireworks — some glitz and glitter, a few pops and bangs and it's gone — while the Church of Christ lasts forever.

We could be in despair if we didn't know that there is a great worldwide outpouring of the Holy Spirit within the Catholic Church. There is, indeed, cause for great courage in these four things:

1. that there is a great number within this state who pray daily for this diocese, its priests and its bishop;

2. that greater is our Lord within his Bride than the power of darkness;

3. the picture of St. George slaying the dragon reminding us that, in the end, Light prevails; and

4. above all, the words of our Lord (the true Power Broker), "I will build my church and the gates of hell will not prevail against it."

May the Holy Spirit pour out a spirit of repentance and true renewal upon us all.

JOE AND RUTH BURKHOLDER
SPOTTSWOOD

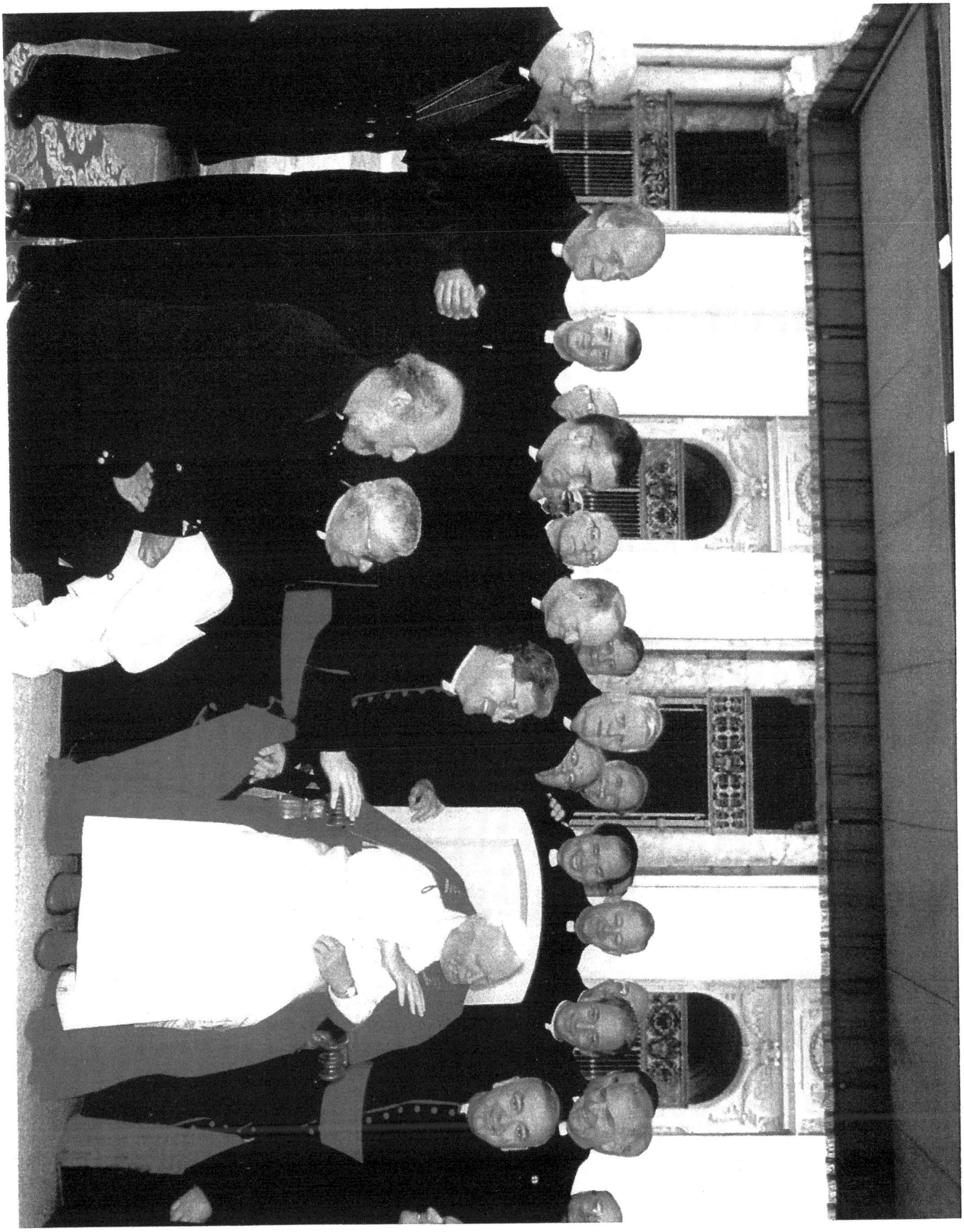

Office of the Bishop *Diocese of Richmond*
811-B CATHEDRAL PLACE • RICHMOND, VIRGINIA 23220-4801 • (804) 359-5661

May 1, 2000

Reverend Thomas J. Quinlan
Blessed. Kateri Tekakwitha Parish
3800 Big Bethel Road
Tabb, VA 23693-3814

Dear T.Q.:

I am pleased to appoint you pastor of Holy Family Parish, Virginia Beach effective as of Monday, June 12. I am appointing Father Larry Mulaney to become the new pastor at Blessed Kateri effective the same date.

I certainly want to thank you for your 12 years of dedicated service to the folks in Poquoson. Blessed Kateri Parish is very much alive and active because of your leadership.

I want to get together with you to discuss your new assignment. May I suggest that we meet for lunch on Friday, May 26 at noontime. I'll be on the Peninsula. I'll even pay for the lunch if you decide where we should eat.

Blessings during the Easter season. I am

Yours sincerely,

+Walter F.

Walter F. Sullivan
Bishop of Richmond

ml

"All the little kids come up to me and say, `T.Q., you've got to stop smoking.'" the Rev. Thomas J. Quinlan says. "I tell them to get the hell out of the way. They're all brainwashed little suburban monsters." Here, he takes a break between Sunday Masses.

"FOOL FOR CHRIST": PRIEST WHOSE BEHAVIOR SOMETIMES SHOCKS BRINGS HIS UNORTHODOX MINISTERIAL WAYS TO BEACH CHURCH

Published: June 24, 2000
Section: DAILY BREAK, page E1
Source: LIZ SZABO, STAFF WRITER
© 2000- Landmark Communications Inc.

SOMEWHERE IN Rome is a file on the Rev. Thomas J. Quinlan. A fat one. And, quite possibly, one of the Vatican's most amusing.

Catholics have been firing off enraged epistles about Quinlan for most of his four decades as a priest. He eats it up. The 71-year-old Quinlan, a chain smoker with a voice like sandpaper, displays the missives as if they are star report cards. "Don't you think Jesus ruffled the feathers of everyone he ever met?" Quinlan asked at his desk, laughing between drags on a cigarette.<
There was the time in 1969 when Quinlan carted off his church's statues to the city dump. "This is not a new concept of Catholicism," an enraged woman wrote to the bishop. "We are victims of vandalism led by a sick man."
That same year, Quinlan held a psychedelic Mass with special lighting effects. Four years later, his priestly orders were nearly suspended when he featured an interpretive dancer at Holy Thursday Mass.
In 1974, a Time magazine profile quoted him calling his parish "spiritual white

trash" who casually drop into Mass to "fill up at God's gas pump."
Quinlan shocked more than a few Catholics when he rode down the center aisle of the Basilica of St. Mary of the Immaculate Conception on a police motorcycle, blue lights flashing, for the Palm Sunday procession.
Jaws dropped, too, when he dressed for Mass on one occasion as Superman, on others as the Grinch or the Blue Angel. And when he led the nearly all-black congregation to Suffolk to re-enact the trial of Nat Turner on Good Friday. And when, at a wedding in 1989, Quinlan went into detail about the sexual imagery invoked by the long, narrow candles used for the liturgy.
"It's not funny," Quinlan said, a mischievous grin folding new creases into his wrinkled face. "It's serious business trying to get people to come to Mass."
Quinlan promises to go easy on his newest parish, the Church of the Holy Family in Virginia Beach. He celebrates his first Mass there tonight. His best friend, Monsignor Thomas J. Caroluzza of Holy Spirit Catholic Church, shakes his head when he imagines how Quinlan's new parishioners will react.
"God help them," said Caroluzza, who was ordained with Quinlan 42 years ago. "It's going to be exciting for Virginia Beach."
Quinlan's friend doubts T.Q., as Quinlan likes to be called, will be able to hold back for very long.
"I'm going to try to be quiet for a while," said Quinlan, who lives like a hermit but swears like a sailor. "Caroluzza gives me two weeks."
Quinlan has a reputation not only for entertaining his flock but also for demanding much from them. At the congregation Quinlan just left, St. Kateri Tekakwitha Catholic Church in Poquosan, Quinlan asked everyone to tithe 5 percent of their income. As a result, Caroluzza said, Quinlan's flock contributed more money every week - an average of $28 each - than any other congregation in the diocese. Most churches average only $5 a week per member.
"His idea is that if you are a committed Catholic, then it's not just a Sunday thing," said Claudette Starrett, a member at St. Kateri. "If he felt like you were slouching, if it appeared to him you were living a lifestyle not commensurate with what you were bringing in, he would call you on it."
Against his congregation's wishes, Quinlan decided to build a church thrift store, Caroluzza said. Now, the members thank him for doing it. The store's proceeds allowed St. Kateri to donate more than $42,000 last year to the poor. The store also provides low-cost clothing to needy people too proud to accept charity, Quinlan said.
As a pastor, Quinlan also sent "red letters" every year at Pentecost to members who hadn't participated in some kind of church ministry. Either start helping, Quinlan told them, or you're out.
Those kinds of demands drive some parishioners away, he acknowledged.
"The new members all bitch about it. Not everybody can take me."
Some Christians are put off by Quinlan's colorful vocabulary, too, Starrett said. After complaints about Quinlan's wedding sermons - particularly his rather earthy advice about the importance of sex in a marriage - some engaged couples chose to "sneak off to another parish" to exchange vows, she said.

Many of the letters on file with the bishop and the papal nuncio include complaints about T.Q.'s salty language from the pulpit.

"I've loosened up a lot," Starrett said. "But I don't think I ever got used to hearing all the sexual innuendo."

Children, especially, aren't sure what to make of T.Q., said Betty Jones, St. Kateri's vacation Bible school director. "When the children are a little bit younger, they're afraid of him," Jones said. "He is kind of scraggly."

And not always patient, as Quinlan himself admits.

"All the little kids come up to me and say, 'T.Q., you've got to stop smoking,' " Quinlan said. "I tell them to get the hell out of the way. They're all brainwashed little suburban monsters."

Quinlan's shock tactics are simply his way of getting people's attention, said church administrator Elaine Riley.

"I wouldn't call it silly," Riley said. "Coming down the aisle on a motorcycle isn't so important compared to having people go home and spend three hours discussing it. . . . Most people go home and they don't remember the homily five minutes out the door. But with T.Q., whether it's negative or positive, he makes you reflect on what you've heard."

St. Kateri, although only 14 years old, now has 850 members. During Quinlan's tenure at St. Mary's in Norfolk, from 1974 to 1985, the congregation tripled in size.

And 1,500 people turned out two years ago to participate in Quinlan's grandest production yet - his own funeral. Or, to be precise, "a pre-funeral gala" on Quinlan's 40th anniversary as a priest. Mourners marched in a long procession led by a New Orleans-style brass bands playing upbeat hymns. Quinlan rode in the hearse.

"You can't talk at your own funeral," said Quinlan, who at over 6-foot-3 is gaunt and haggard but still kicking. "I wanted to talk at mine."

Caroluzza belted out "Don't Cry for Me, Church of Richmond," to the tune of the theme song from "Evita." Even Bishop Walter F. Sullivan, who has long tolerated Quinlan's antics, read a poem called "An Ode to the Blue Angel."

It was only at about the time of Quinlan's mock funeral that he began revealing his real age, Caroluzza said. "Each time he's moved, he's taken another year off his age," said the monsignor, the regional vicar for southeastern Virginia. "He only started telling the truth when he hit 68, because he knows you can only retire at 70."

T.Q. dismisses the idea of stepping down from the priesthood. "What would I do - retire and write dirty novels?"

But Quinlan is more than just a jokester, Caroluzza said. He is, in the words of St. Paul, a "**fool** for **Christ**" - a label that Quinlan relishes as a great compliment.

"If it were just zaniness, it would be one hijink after another," Caroluzza said. "The zany stories are the only ones people remember. They don't remember his visiting the sick. That's the real T.Q."

If Quinlan refuses to behave, Caroluzza said, it's partly to avoid "playing footsie with authority." The mischievous priest is determined to stay on the margins, to avoid the trappings and temptations of power.

"His quirks offend some people," Starrett said, "but he's just very human. He doesn't want to be put on a pedestal."

Quinlan's congregants feel free, too, to speak their minds, Starrett said. They confront him when they think he's gone too far. And they intervene when they see him in serious trouble.

Quinlan, like so many artistic personalities, has a drinking problem. Alcoholism runs in his family, and Quinlan has battled the problem since he was a teen-ager, Caroluzza said. The bishop has sent him to alcohol counseling in the past. In newspaper interviews in the 1980s, the priest said that he had been able to quit.

But last year, Quinlan was convicted of driving under the influence of alcohol. He was fined $250 and referred to an alcohol recovery program. Quinlan didn't want to talk about the conviction, but he said that on that occasion he was only driving a few hundred feet to a store. He hasn't had a drink since September, he said.

Starrett said her priest's problem is well-known.

"It's part of his humanness," she said. "Some people can't accept that from a priest. . . . It's a disease. But some people don't see it as a disease. They see it as a frailty - particularly in a priest - and think that's worse."

Congregants such as Jones say they appreciate Quinlan's honesty. "There's no way you can keep this quiet," she said. "He's very upfront. . . . He's working on it."

Caroluzza said Quinlan was both humble and courageous when facing up to his parish.

"He went to his congregation and said, `I can leave.' They said, `We don't want you to leave. We want you to change,' " Caroluzza said. "His community really loved him. They loved him into sobriety."

He's only been gone a few days, but many at St. Kateri miss Quinlan already. Jones has a feeling that Quinlan's reputation has preceded him to Holy Family. She envies that parish, though, for its chance to be with her old pastor.

"I hope they give him a chance," she said. "Learn to love him the way the rest of us do. He's a good man, with a good heart, an intelligent man who can teach them a lot."

Some who attend Holy Family don't know what to expect.

"When it comes to church, this is the word of the Lord and it should be respected with utmost dignity," said Tom Pauls. "If this guy comes in on a motorcycle, I'm going to find another church."

Others are looking forward to the adventure.

"I think he'll be a tremendous asset to the parish," said Dan Creedon, who also has not yet met his new pastor. "I know that he's very dedicated to the poor. That's what the church is about."

Quinlan knows that it may take time for his parish to get used to him. His most loyal fans always come 20 years after he's left, he said. And, these days, it's getting harder and harder to shock anyone.

"I'm the age now that I can do no wrong," Quinlan said. "It's sort of sad."

Quinlan blesses Frank Kmetz

The Rev. Thomas Quinlan leads a prayer at Church of the Holy Family in Virginia Beach, his new parish.

Reach Liz Szabo by calling 446-2286 or online at lszabo(AT)pilotonline.com

Quinlan Quips
On life after death, in a 1981 interview:
"There's just God and me and you. No devil. No angels. But there is a heaven, and Jesus is in it. And I can't wait to get there."
On his inattention to his health:
"People ask me `Who's your doctor?' I say, `Franklin Funeral Home.'"
On the Rosary:
"I hate the Rosary."
On his priorities as a Catholic:
"To me, if you don't serve the poor, then forget it."

"The sermon could be seven minutes longer or 27 minutes. If I don't like the bride and groom, I'll talk even longer."
On himself:
"I hope I haven't scandalized you. I wouldn't mind if I did."
On being a free-thinker:
"When you come to the Catholic church and dip your finger in the holy water, don't throw your brains out at the same time."
On the design of his last church:
"I hired a Jewish architect. I told him, "If you make it look like a church, I'll kill you."
Recommendation for his epitaph:
"He was odd."

© 2000- Virginian-Pilot

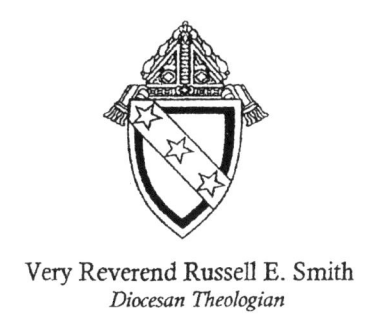

Diocese of Richmond

Office of the Diocesan Theologian
811 Cathedral Place • Richmond, VA 23220-4801

Very Reverend Russell E. Smith
Diocesan Theologian

March 24, 2005

Reverend Thomas Quinlan
Church of the Holy Family
1279 N. Great Neck Road
Virginia Beach, VA 23454

Dear TQ,

Bishop DiLorenzo received the enclosed letter from Mr. Malcolm D'Souza, with his observations about the way the liturgy is celebrated at Holy Family. Would you kindly look over this letter and tell me if the points he raises are true.

I am sorry to bring this matter to your attention during Holy week. As the entire spirit of the liturgy should have us attending to other matters; nevertheless, the Bishop is interested in your response to the points made by Mr. D'Souza. If we could hear from you by April 15th I would really appreciate it. Thanks very much for your attention to these matters.

Sincerely yours in Christ,

The Very Reverend Russell E. Smith, S.T.D.
Diocesan Theologian

Phone: (804) 359-5661 • Fax: (804) 358-9159

March 7, 2005

The Most Reverend Francis Xavier DiLorenzo, D.D., S.T.D.,
Bishop of the Catholic Diocese of Richmond
811 Cathedral Place
Richmond, VA 23220-4801

Your Excellency,

Hoping this letter finds you in the best of health and happiness in your new diocese.

It is with grave concern, however, I write this letter. I am a parishioner of Blessed Sacrament Catholic Church in Alexandria, Virginia in the Arlington Diocese. I used to be an altar boy as a youth, and I am currently an Extraordinary Minister of Communion. My wife and I continue to remain members in good standing with our parish and our Roman Catholic Church. It is after deep prayer and reflection that I write this letter to you in regards to Reverend Father Thomas Quinlan, a priest and a pastor of the Church of the Holy Family in Virginia Beach in your Richmond Diocese.

While visiting relatives in Virginia Beach, we attended "mass" at his church on February 13, of this year. My wife and I were taken aback at the manner which Fr. Quinlan "celebrated mass." His unusual style was certainly not in line with a normal mass that we have come to know in our adult Catholic lives. Fr. Quinlan tailored the sacred mass to his desire. Plainly speaking, Fr. Quinlan does not follow the guidelines prescribed by the US Catholic Bishops nor the Holy See. And the most egregious act committed by this priest is the fact that he did not say the Eucharistic prayer during the consecration of the Most Precious Body and Blood of Jesus as instructed, thus making his mass invalid and a sacrilege. Fr. Quinlan strayed from the directed prayer, and used another "prayer" including consecrating the bread and wine. This behavior shocked us, and left us quite troubled.

In addition to this most scandalous act mentioned, Fr. Quinlan performed several other exploits during the mass that I consider disrespectful and again not in line with our universal Mother Church. I do indeed understand these items below committed by Fr. Quinlan and the parishioners make the sacred mass "illicit not invalid," but certainly believe are noteworthy in mentioning:

- During his homily, Fr. Quinlan referred to the second reading of St. Paul as "horrendous." He went on to describe the mixing of St. Paul's writings in the Catholic and Protestant churches as a whole bunch of "S-H-I-T" - actually spelling this swear word, a profanity, while addressing the congregation which included children. He also insisted that angels and devils do not exist as they are "myths" written in the Bible, and in referring to Sunday's Gospel, Jesus went to the desert simply for an examination of conscience, and was not tempted by Satan as the Gospel clearly states.

- After the homily, Fr. Quinlan stated that we would say the Apostles Creed instead of the Nicene Creed because it was "simple creed instead of saying the other one."

- After the General Intercessions, for the offertory, several members of the congregation brought the bread in glass bowls and the wine in wine glasses and placed them on the altar with no corporeal on the altar. Fr. Quinlan did not receive them, and he did not say any of the offertory prayers nor the "Preparation of the Gifts" including the fact that he did not add the water to the wine nor wash his hands. He went directly to the prayer thereafter i.e. "Lord be with you"

- After the Sanctus, as there is plenty of room to kneel, the parishioners remained standing as there are no kneelers. The floor was of hard concrete, however, my wife and I knelt on her jacket. Fr. Quinlan, as mentioned above, continued with a prayer that was not indeed the actual prayer of consecration.

- After the "Eucharistic prayers," he raised the bread and wine, and Fr. Quinlan invited everyone to recite the Doxology (Through Him, with him etc) along with him.

- For Our Lord's Prayer, Fr. Quinlan left the sanctuary/altar, and came down and joined hands with the people in the first row facing the altar.

- During communion, Fr. Quinlan did not distribute communion to the Extraordinary Ministers of Communion until after the congregation had received. The communion as I was told, since I did not receive it, was made of brittle and flaky pieces of bread.

- After communion, all of the bread was joined together into one bowl and the wine into one wine glass, and the Extraordinary Ministers of Communion returned them to the back of the church – without consuming the Precious Blood. I am unsure of where they had taken it as I did not observe a tabernacle or reservation chapel area.

After mass was completed, I was truly distressed and very bothered by the fact that I had not attended or participated in a "true sacred" mass in every sense of the words. I was annoyed by the lack of respect given to the holy mass and decided that I would indeed speak with Fr. Quinlan. However, when I discussed with him the way he celebrated his "mass," Fr. Quinlan was immediately agitated, and felt he was indeed in line with the church. I explained to him while I was kneeling, after the Sanctus, he did not state the proper words of consecration. Fr. Quinlan claimed he had said Eucharistic Prayer II, one that I am very familiar with and I assured him that he certainly did not follow, especially with regards to the words of consecration. He continued to state that I should not have been kneeling as I too am "a priest." Fr. Quinlan, in my opinion, is confusing the ministerial priesthood to which he belongs and the universal or common priesthood to which we all belong through our baptism. Out of respect, I ended our conversation and left the church. I returned to my parish in Alexandria that evening, and attended a true sacred mass.

As you are able to see, Your Excellency, I was quite concerned by the entire incident, and I have prayed and reflected over it for several weeks. It is disturbing to me that Fr. Quinlan leads a parish, and celebrates mass to satisfy his own whims in regards to how the sacrifice of mass should be celebrated. All the while he makes the "mass" invalid for the parishioners who may not know any better. This incident prompted me to write this letter to you that you may be aware of the atrocity occurring by a pastor in a parish within your diocese. I bring this to your attention in hopes that you will do what is necessary to correct at the very least the invalidity of the sacred mass.

In addition to prayer and reflection, I have discussed this incident with my pastor of Blessed Sacrament Catholic Church - Reverend Father John Cregan, to whom I have copied this letter. It is not in attempting to spread this occurrence around, but to receive guidance that I related it to him.

I continue to pray for Fr. Quinlan and the parishioners of his church, for you and your new diocese, and for our Roman Catholic Church, that Our Lord Jesus Christ, who is Our Hope and Our Light, may bless each of us and keep us always as a one, holy, Catholic and apostolic Church in His tender care.

Sincerely,

Malcolm D'Souza

CC: Rev. Fr. John C. Cregan, Pastor
Blessed Sacrament Catholic Church

CC: Rev. Fr. Thomas Quinlan, Pastor
Church of the Holy Family

April 10, 2005

Most Rev. Francis X. DiLorenzo
811 Cathedral Place
Richmond, Virginia 23220

Dear Bishop DiLorenzo:

I am responding to your letter concerning the observations of Mr. Malcolm D'Souza of Alexandria, Virginia, a visitor to Holy Family on the first Sunday in Lent, February 13, 2005.

1. I am afraid that some of the responses will have to be "I-said–he-heard:" unless I can re-assemble the 600 witnesses of this particular Mass.

During Lent I always use Eucharistic Prayer II because of its brevity in light of the longer readings of this holy season. I never veer from the words of the Canon except adding the words, least of all the Words of Institution or the Epiclesis. This would make the Mass invalid. Now and then I add the words, "following Jewish custom". But the Introduction to the Roman Missal gives us some leeway by noting: "The priest may say something like this". Also it should be pointed out to Mr. D'Souza, who seems to be a fundamentalist Catholic, that the Words of Institution themselves are a paraphrase of Scripture.

2. As to the homily, this is really a case of what I said and what he heard. I said that the second reading was horrendous because it distracted terribly from the message of this important day in the liturgical year. I wouldn't even think of calling St. Paul's writings horrendous in themselves. As to my saying Jesus examined h8is conscience or something like that is silly. I spoke of this being classically viewed as a retreat before His ministry began, and how we should imitate Him. Re: the angels and devils involved in the Gospel I exhorted the people to be aware of the Matthean construct, and not to be envisioning a devil zooming Jesus around Jerusalem like Superman or E. T. I didn't use the word myth in this context!

3. At Creed time I introduce it by saying "Following an ancient Tradition, and in support of our catechumens during this season, let us recite our Creed. In #137 of GIRM it does not specify which Creed is to be recited albeit the Nicene Creed seems to be implied. We would need direction from your diocesan liturgical commission on this.

4. As to not reciting the Offertory prayers ALOUD #142, par. 2 of GIRM states the opposite: "If there is no Offertory chant, the priest MAY say them aloud." We always have an Offertory, or better, a Preparation of the Gifts' song.

I do not think Mr. D'Souza understands that the Offertory (the offering of Jesus to the Father) takes place later in the Mass.

As to the glass bowls and chalices, and the People of God setting their own table, I will speak of this later on in this letter.

5. As to kneeling during the Eucharistic Prayer this is a serious problem at Holy Family because of the materials in the floor and the construct of the people itself. In our gradual implementation of GIRM, we are preparing to bring this problem to your diocesan liturgical commission We have eighteen nonagenarians and almost two-hundred octogenarians, not to mention several hundred septuagenarians in this parish. Not only could they not kneel, but now many of them have to sit during the Eucharistic Prayer because of their debilities.

6. My not distributing Communion during Mass. That particular Sunday I was recovering from the flu. Not to mention that there was a priest as the lead distributor of the Eucharist, Fr. James Connelly, a Navy chaplain, who often con-celebrants here when he cannot get on base.

7. After Mass Mr. D'Souza came to the door of the sacristy and with his child as a veritable shield blocked the door to others, making no complaint to me, merely asking if this were a Jesuit church. My agitation came from the fact that six or seven people were waiting to speak to me, not to mention the Book Store minister waving her hands at me, trying to signal that she needed to get into the sacristy to extricate the money box for same.

8. As to Mr. D'Souza's not receiving the Eucharist because of our Bread. He didn't eat it. How could he know?. Our recipe is diocesan approved. There is nothing brittle or flaky about it. This is a rash judgement. The sacrilege here is a person coming to Mass without receiving the Sacred Body and Blood of Our Lord. We seem to have a reversal of values. Rubrics are ancillary to the celebration, not the opposite

9. Now as to what seems to be the main concern of Mr. D'Soluza, sc. The implementation of GIRM.

We at Holy Family have been studying assiduously the new rubrics of GIRM, and have finally adopted a step-by-step implementation with accompanying catechesis. You must remember as a seminarian all the unnecessary confusion after the promulgation of the Constitution on the Sacred Liturgy. Not to mention in your Philadelphia experience Cardinal Krol's non-implementation of turning the altars around, and then the stories about his non implementation of Saturday night Masses which caused hundreds to drive over to Camden, New Jersey. We hope to avoid this.

As a result each Sunday we put into force various new rubrics:

We have already stopped leaving the altar for the Kiss Of Peace.

This Sunday we will have removed the glass chalices and are using the ones made by Dr. Trimble – silver/metallic chalices, which we had stored. (He was a retired doctor who went with his wife as a missionary to Nicaragua in the 70s). We have ordered nine silver patens.

The corporals have arrived from Belgium. To tell you the truth I had never averted to the lack of a corporal here because of the heavy linen altar cloth.

By July 1 GIRM should be fully implemented in this parish. I think this is admirable. Many other parishes are betwixt and between and perplexed. (I have received copies of letters from nineteen fellow priests who were "reported" as not following GIRM). Maybe we need more direction and a timetable from your diocesan liturgical commission.

My slow implementation may of GIRM may be a scandal to Mr. D'Souza, but his not receiving Eucharist of validly consecrated Bread and Wine is more of a scandal!

With every best wish, I remain

Sincerely yours in Our Lord.

(Rev.) Thomas J. Quinlan

cc: Rev. Monsignor Thomas J. Caroluzza, Vicar - Eastern Vicariate
    Very Rev. Russell E. Smith, S. T. D., Diocesan Theologian

Diocese of Richmond

Chancery Office • 811 Cathedral Place, Richmond, Virginia 23220-4801 • Phone: (804) 359-5661 • Fax: (804) 358-9159

Office of the Bishop

Rev. Thomas Quinlan
Church of the Holy Family
1279 N. Great Neck Road
Virginia Beach, VA 23454

Dear Tom:

I appreciate the time we spent meeting together on Friday, April 15th with the outcome being that I am retiring you.

As you know, the diocesan policy states that the normal age for retirement for priests is 70 years of age, and you are well beyond that. After reviewing your records and given the advice of my advisers, I made the decision that you should retire, not from ministry, but from administration. We look forward to your continued participation in the life of the Diocese in the years to come.

In terms of your living situation, please check with Mark Lane if you need any help or assistance.

If you have any questions about your retirement benefits, please call on Etta Shepperd, our Benefits specialist here in the Chancery Office.

Lastly, I want to commend you, and on behalf of the people of God, I want to thank you for your many years of service in the Diocese of Richmond.

With every best wish, I remain,

Sincerely yours in Our Lord,

+ Francis X. DiLorenzo
Most Rev. Francis X. DiLorenzo
Bishop of Richmond

April 18, 2005

A DIOCESE IN WANT OF PRIESTS

Push for Beach pastor to retire underscores problems of an aging clergy

BY STEVEN G. VEGH
THE VIRGINIAN-PILOT

VIRGINIA BEACH — Gruff, opinionated and iconoclastic doesn't begin to describe the Rev. Thomas J. Quinlan, the gravel-voiced, chain-smoking priest of Holy Family Catholic Church in Virginia Beach. During his 47 years of parish ministry, "TQ" scorned public opinion – and doctrine as well, critics say – in colorfully preaching his interpretation of Vatican II Catholicism.

Quinlan advocated vigorous lay involvement in the Mass and ministry, and salted services with attention-grabbing twists, such as a famous Palm Sunday motorcycle ride in the sanctuary of the Basilica of St. Mary of the Immaculate Conception in Norfolk

But his days as a priest in charge of a parish are numbered. After receiving a complaint from a visitor to Holy Family about the priest's unorthodoxy, Bishop Francis X. DiLorenzo wrote to "strongly suggest" that Quinlan retire.

"I had a visit with him and told him I wanted another year and he said, 'No, I'm retiring you,'" Quinlan said last week after talking with the bishop. About 900 parishioners have signed a letter to DiLorenzo appealing his decision. The priest's supporters say there's room

Continued on Page A12

The Rev. Thomas J. Quinlan, the unorthodox pastor at Holy Family Catholic Church in Virginia Beach, was told by the Catholic Diocese of Richmond that it "strongly" suggests he retire.

The Rev. William L. Pitt, principal of Bishop Sullivan Catholic High School at the Beach, led a panel to study the priest-shortage problem.

Continued from Page A1

enough in the faith for him and they can't understand how a diocese with a shortage of clergy can afford to let him go.

The controversy is threatening to eclipse, at least temporarily, a longer-term problem facing Holy Family and many other parishes in the Catholic Diocese of Richmond: the aging of the clergy.

Quinlan is 76, one of at least 39 priests in the diocese who are in their 60s or older. In preparation for their inevitable retirement or deaths, and with few replacements in the pipeline, the diocese has recently been relinquishing its one-priest-per-parish tradition.

What may become the new norm: one priest per two or three "clustered" parishes.

The change was among the remedies suggested by the Commission for Pastoral Planning, which began studying the diocese's chronic clergy shortage last fall.

"In the past, the norm was that a parish or a congregation exists alone, and that can't be the norm anymore," said the commission's director, the Rev. William L. Pitt, who is planning to retire this summer. He is the principal of Bishop Sullivan Catholic High School in Virginia Beach.

Pitt said the commission has also recommended that the diocese vastly increase training and educational programs that would equip parishioners to take over certain roles from priests that don't require clergy credentials.

"It would offer parishes some vibrant ministry," Pitt said. "It's what lay people are called to do, whether priests are here or not, or even if we had an abundance of priests."

It's not clear whether the next priest at Holy Family would have responsibilities for another parish. DiLorenzo, who could not be reached for an interview, hasn't announced which parishes are candidates for clustering. The bishop has clustered two Richmond parishes, St. Patrick's and St. Peter's, in the past year.

The Rev. Thomas J. Quinlan, 76, is one of at least 39 priests in the Catholic Diocese of Richmond who are in their 60s or older. Retirements will leave the diocese with a priest shortage and may end the diocese's one-priest-per-parish tradition.

At Holy Family, parishioners are still hoping DiLorenzo will change his mind about Quinlan and let the priest stay one more year to complete his regular six-year term. "He's essentially led Holy Family into Catholic revival," said John Owens, a former Navy pilot. "It is now a place where people are on fire in service for Christ and the Catholic mission."

Whether DiLorenzo is willing to reverse his decision should be known later this month when he announces the transfers and new posting of priests to parishes; the assignments take effect on June 13. There are more parish vacancies than priests.

Many Catholic lay leaders in Hampton Roads strongly expect that some local parishes will be clustered.

Clustering is a strategy DiLorenzo endorsed as the bishop of the Diocese of Honolulu, where he served for 10 years before coming to Richmond last May.

The nationwide priest shortage is rooted in a nosedive in ordinations that followed the social upheaval of the 1960s and the new Catholic policies and practices promulgated at that time by the Second Vatican Council.

According to the Center for Applied Research in the Apostolate at Georgetown University, the United States had nearly 36,000 diocesan priests in 1965. There were 28,967 in 2004. During the same period, the country's Catholic population rose from 45.6 million to 64.3 million.

The Richmond Diocese has also suffered in the past from a lack of new, "homegrown" priests. There were no ordinations in the diocese in 2002, one in 2003, none in 2004 and one in 2005. Four ordinations are expected in 2006 and two in 2007.

To boost vocations, the bishop has assigned the Rev. Michael Renninger to be the diocese's full-time vocations director. Renninger, who had already worked part time in that role, said that by next fall, the diocese will have 17 seminarians working toward ordination, which he called a good number for the diocese's size. The diocese, which encompasses southern Virginia from the Appalachians to the Eastern Shore, has about 218,000 members and 145 parishes.

To cope with low vocations, the Richmond Diocese has relied partly on priests from overseas to fill parish vacancies. Priests who are "on loan" from dioceses in the Philippines are particularly common.

But even the use of foreign priests hasn't offset the problem of an American priesthood crowded with men who are approaching or are past retirement age.

In the Richmond Diocese as of last fall, six of the 111 active priests were 70 or older, and 13 were between and 69. Twenty were between 60 and 64, and 52 were in their 50s. Only 20 were younger than 50 years old, and only three of them were younger than 40, according to the latest statistics available from the diocese's Pastoral Planning Committee. The statistics were published last December in The Catholic Virginian, the diocese's official newspaper.

Priests can retire upon reaching age 70, and three of the four South Hampton Roads priests currently scheduled to retire in June are that age, or older: Quinlan, Pitt, and the Rev. Thomas Caroluzza, the pastor of Blessed Sacrament Catholic Church in Norfolk and the bishop's representative in eastern Virginia. The latter two have said they are retiring voluntarily.

The Rev. John J. Dorgan of the Basilica of St. Mary in Norfolk, is retiring for health reasons. He is 65. At least one other diocesan priest, in Hopewell, is also retiring, according to Stephen S. Neil, editor of The Catholic Virginian.

For Hampton Roads parishes that may be clustered, Southwest Virginia may be a good place to look for what to expect. Priest-sharing is a reality at St. Joseph Catholic Church in Woodlawn, All Saints Catholic Church in Floyd and Church of the Risen Lord in Patrick Springs. Juan Rios, a founding member of St. Joseph, said All Saints and Risen Lord are small "mission" congregations that have never had their own priest.

Rios said his priest has a killing schedule" that involves celebrating Mass at two different churches on Sunday. The third congregation, All Saints, has no Sunday service – Communion is only available on Saturday.

When the priest is sick or out of town, the congregations rely on a permanent deacon who can perform some, but not all, of the sacraments. "I think it is better than nothing," Rios said.

Pitt acknowledged that if clustering and priest-sharing spreads, more Catholics face the possibility that their church might have fewer Sunday Masses, or perhaps no Sunday Eucharistic service at all.

"That's a major change, that's a change in our undergirding," he said. Only priests can consecrate the bread and wine for Communion, which is the defining ritual of Catholicism.

In Portsmouth, St. Paul Catholic Church members are aware they could be clustered, perhaps with Church of the Holy Angels in Portsmouth and St. Mary Catholic Church in Chesapeake. The Pastoral Planning Committee discussed the priest shortage and likely remedies with church leaders around the diocese last fall.

"We don't know whether we're going to share a priest, although we suspect that will be the case," said John Shine Jr., the president of St. Paul's parish council.

For some parishioners, and elderly members particularly, the prospect is scary and unwanted, said Shine, an accountant with a 23-year history at St. Paul.

Yet Shine is hopeful that if clustering occurs, his co-parishioners can rise to the occasion and take on more responsibilities, as some priest-sharing parishes have in western Virginia. Such parishes even distribute Communion, using "elements" previously consecrated by a priest.

Shine is also optimistic that with clustering, his 181-year-old congregation could adopt a new, broader definition of what it means to belong to a church.

"It would be a mind-set change that we are a parish greater than St. Paul," he said. "That we are a Catholic community, and I just happen to go to this building for worship and register at this parish."

Even Owens, a leader in the "Save TQ" campaign at Holy Family, acknowledged at a meeting last week that the parish's future was not bound up in Quinlan's fate.

"We are the church," he said in the modern sanctuary as several hundred parishioners brooded and listened. "TQ is not the church, and his absence should not stop us. We need to move on and do good things, and honor TQ in that way."

■ *Reach Steven G. Vegh at (757) 446-2417 or* steven.vegh@pilotonline.com.

DIOCESE'S AGING PRIESTS

The Catholic Diocese of Richmond is top-heavy with aging priests whose retirement or death could worsen an already chronic clergy shortage. One likely remedy is for certain parishes to share a single priest, an arrangement known as "clustering."

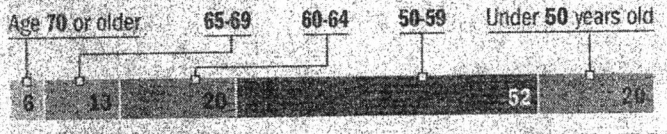

Age 70 or older	65-69	60-64	50-59	Under 50 years old
6	13	20	52	20

SOURCE: Pastoral Planning Committee, Diocese of Richmond — The Virginian-Pilot

Article - Parishioners were ignored

Publication: The Virginian-Pilot, **Section:** Hampton Roads, **Page:** 22, **Date:** Wednesday, May 04, 2005

Parishioners were ignored

As parishioners of Holy Family Church in Virginia Beach, we appreciate your focus on the blow that has been leveled against our parish by Bishop DiLorenzo of the Richmond diocese in summarily dismissing our beloved pastor, the Rev. Thomas Quinlan (aka TQ).

More than 900 parishioners signed an appeal to the bishop to permit this devoted man of God to fulfill his final year of revitalizing this once sleepy parish into the dynamic ministry that TQ has brought about. The bishop deigned not to reply personally to our appeal but foisted the job of rejecting it onto his secretary.

As your article points out, the severe shortage of priests has the diocese heading toward "clustering" parishes without priests yet turns this good man out to pasture because he has reached age 76. Pope Benedict XVI, at 78, need beware.

But the greatest affront in this tawdry episode is the manner in which we Holy Family parishioners were shoved aside by the bishop with no consultation whatsoever.

Father Quinlan has been recognized as controversial throughout his 47 years of devoted service in the priesthood. He has "afflicted the comfortable and comforted the afflicted." He often "fires for effect" from the pulpit and we understand his purpose.

But his primary focus has been on the poor and disenfranchised and the sick. The tithing program he instituted has virtually eliminated the enormous debt he inherited on arrival here. His accomplishments in service to the migrant workers on the Eastern Shore and to our sister parish in Haiti are legion.

Certainly we realize that our parish will survive without our pastor because of the motivation he has instilled in us. However, the shabby treatment we parishioners received from the bishop and the diocese makes us wonder if the Vatican II Council ever took place.

The diocese has suggested that the Rev. Quinlan retire.

Dan Creedon and Bob Horan
Virginia Beach

Reader upset by priest's retirement

I am writing in regard to the recent request from Bishop DiLorenzo retiring Father Thomas Quinlan, pastor of the Church of the Holy Family in Virginia Beach. It seems the reason for this decision was a letter sent to the bishop by a visiting Catholic from northern Virginia complaining about Father Quinlan.

The letter cited trivial details from the Mass, many of which were purely matters of opinion. For example, the Eucharist was called "brittle and flaky," despite the fact that the man refused to receive the Communion. It deeply concerns me that Father Quinlan was chastised (by the man who wrote the bishop) for leaving the altar during the Sign of Peace in order to form a circle of unity with his congregation for the Lord's Prayer.

As a 15-year-old Catholic quickly approaching Confirmation, I was greatly troubled that a man outside our parish could have such a large effect on our spiritual lives. Although Father Quinlan has offended some people, including myself at times, I have learned very much about our faith during the five years that he has been at our parish.

I personally do not believe that a man outside our parish should have the right to influence such a weighty decision that affects the lives of so many faithful parishioners at Holy Family.

Erin L. Convery
Virginia Beach

UNIVERSITY OF NOTRE DAME
DEPARTMENT OF THEOLOGY
130 MALLOY HALL
NOTRE DAME • INDIANA • 46556-4619

REV. RICHARD P. McBRIEN
CROWLEY-O'BRIEN PROFESSOR OF THEOLOGY
tel. 574-631-5151 or 631-7811 fax 574-631-4169
rmcbrien@nd.edu

May 5, 2005

Dear TQ:

    I have just been informed of your enforced retirement as pastor of Holy Family parish. I believe that you knew this to be a distinct possibility, given the profile of the new bishop. It is ironic nonetheless that, in this time of an acute shortage of active priests, a bishop would order into retirement a pastor like yourself who has amply demonstrated an extraordinary vigor and dedication to his ministry and has evoked from his parishioners almost universal appreciation and deep affection.

    I can say all this as one who has experienced the situation at first-hand, having observed and felt the dynamism of the parish and its members. Indeed, I have been profoundly impressed with their commitment to ministry of every kind and with their evident determination to contribute financially and in so many other ways to support their faith-community's outreach to those in need, whether within the parish or beyond it. For this, you deserve--but do not expect or desire--a full measure of credit.

    For what it is worth, TQ, I salute you at this transitional moment in your pastoral life, knowing full well that, while it may involve a retirement from office in the canonical sense of the word, it will almost certainly not be a retirement from pastoral ministry and service to the Church. I am confident that the bishop will not have heard or seen the last of you in the Diocese of Richmond. I surely hope not, because not only the diocese but the wider Church will continue to need your independent and creative spirit for as long as there is life and health in you.

                                     Warm regards always,

                                      Dick

Letters

Complaint on Fr. Quinlan not isolated incident

I read in the May 9 Catholic Virginian a letter from Erin Convery, an articulate and disappointed 15-year-old parishioner at Holy Family (Virginia Beach). She is upset about the Bishop asking the Pastor, Fr. Quinlan, to retire. Erin mentioned a visitor's letter complaining about what he'd experienced as Fr. Quinlan presided over Mass at Holy Family. Erin apparently believes that this one letter caused the Bishop's action — she mentioned it three times in that one short letter.

I'm writing to set the record straight for those who, like Erin, believe that this is an isolated incident. It happened at least one other time in the few years that Fr. Quinlan has been pastor at Holy Family. A visitor from Texas wrote a letter to the Bishop (Walter F. Sullivan) in the summer of 2002 in which he cited several theological and doctrinal offenses in the pastor's homily and called Fr. Quinlan a heretic for speaking them.

The pastor's response to that letter was printed in the bulletin and that response caused yet another controversy for its harsh tone. I intended to refer Erin and others to the parish web site to read those words for themselves. Curiously, out of the scores of notes available there, only those related to that incident seem to have been removed.

I understand from a parishioner who has known Fr. Quinlan for decades that these kinds of things have gone on all those years and that the Diocese and the Vatican have fat files documenting them. We can't know if the Bishop's decision was based on this kind of controversy alone, which I doubt, but this was, by no means, an isolated incident of one visitor sending one angry letter.

All that said, Fr. Quinlan has been a true minister to the sick, the poor and all of us, as other letters have noted. Our food for the poor program has grown dramatically since Fr. Quinlan

See LETTERS page 9

Letters

Continued from page 6

arrived. He single-handedly got our Haiti Parish Twinning program started and has encouraged this affluent parish to give an astounding amount of money which is being used to transform not just the poor St. Jude parish, but the entire town of Baptiste. It's a shame that, with all of his blessings, those parishioners who believe what's in the Catechism of the Catholic Church and participate in Mass every weekend find themselves wincing repeatedly at his "teachings" and have to explain his PG-13 rated homilies to their children on the way home.

Lon Scofield
Virginia Beach

Man laments many abuses in liturgy

I am writing in response to the letter in your May 9th edition from Erin Convery, a young member of Holy Family Parish (Virginia Beach), who expressed her distress over the retirement of Fr. Thomas Quinlan as that parish's pastor.

Her letter joined a host of others recently published in the Virginian Pilot that not only expressed similar bewilderment, but angrily attacked Bishop DiLorenzo for a host of "offenses," from not consulting with the parish, or not being in the "spirit of Vatican II," to "needing to search for a soul," as one lady astonishingly wrote. There does not seem to be a single dissenting voice to be found in the uproar over the Bishop's decision. Please record my dissent, and allow me to express my sadness at the misguided focus.

A few months ago, as I began to question the celebration of the liturgy at another Virginia Beach parish that I am a member of, I had my eyes opened to the considerable liturgical abuse that was prevalent in my own parish, and in many parishes in the surrounding area.

The document on the Sacred Liturgy produced during Vatican II (Sacrosanctum Concilium) states that the regulation of the Sacred Liturgy depends solely on the authority of the Church, and that no one, not even a priest, can change, add to, or subtract from, the Sacred Liturgy on their own authority.(SC 22). The "Spirit of Vatican II," does not mean "Anything Goes."

Can we honestly say that as the Universal Church, we universally are obedient to that precept? If we were, then letters of complaint from visitors would not be required. These are not "trivial details," as Miss Convery tries to minimize the chaos in our liturgy.

There should be no "large effect on our spiritual lives," based on who is the Celebrant or pastor, because they all are supposed to be celebrating the Sacred Liturgy of the Church the same way. The faithful should not have to "shop" for the church that "feels right."

What we have instead is a variety of liturgical "practices," depending on the orthodoxy of the particular pastor, liturgical committee, music minister, etc. Why else would we have some churches built without kneelers, despite the prescribed norm for the entire United States to kneel during the Consecration as a sign of reverence to the Real Presence, while another church a few miles away has kneelers and the tabernacle still in a place of honor?

Why do we have some priests who do not genuflect at the Consecration, or wash their hands at the Preparation of the Gifts, or wear proper vestments, while down the street a reverent priest is obediently and faithfully celebrating the Holy Sacrifice of the Mass, the Church's Liturgy, in the Person of Christ, according to the Missal and liturgical books?

Why, despite an instruction from the Vatican intended to stop abuses of the Holy Eucharist (Redemptionis Sacramentum) do we still observe the same abuses repeated week after week, as if some of us simply know better, and the hierarchy simply doesn't "get it?"

For me, it comes down to a few fundamental truths that I too was adrift on just a couple months ago. First and foremost is belief in the Real Presence. Sadly, polls show most Catholics no longer believe in transubstantiation, and the Real Presence of Christ in both the Eucharist at Mass, and in the tabernacle.

This erosion of belief is manifested in some of the liturgical abuses mentioned above that drain the Mass of its sacred nature, and erroneously shifts focus "horizontally" on Christ's presence in the community of "celebrants," and the Eucharist as a "shared meal," rather than the "vertical" adoration of Jesus in the Most Blessed Sacrament. This is not the teaching of the Holy Catholic Church, yet most of us don't even recognize how we have drifted.

If we truly believe, then why would reverence be scorned by some of the faithful as something belonging in the "dark ages" of the Church? And finally, if we believe as we say in the Creed in "one Holy, Catholic and Apostolic Church," then why is fidelity to the teachings of the Church, including how the Sacrifice of the Mass is supposed to be celebrated universally by Christ's Mystical Bride, not worthy of our faithful trust? If we don't believe, then instead of trying to change the Church, why be Catholic?

John D. Paul
Virginia Beach

Tidewater priests will be missed

I agree with Anne Prince's letter (CV, May 9) that certain priests from our Tidewater area, who are retiring will be missed.

We are fortunate to have several up-and-coming priests, who have served us, who are making positive strides also — Father Russell Smith, Msgr. Walter Barrett and Father James Gordon to name a few.

May God bless and reward all the priests from our diocese who make a difference.

Mary Allen
Norfolk

Fr. Quinlan lauded for building faith

The last edition of The Catholic Virginian carried biosketches of five retiring priests. All evidenced inspiring examples of dedication and service. As a member of Holy Family parish, I wish to speak further about Rev. T. J. Quinlan, our pastor.

After 12 years of Catholic grade and high school and university education, I believed I had a reasonably well grounded Catholic faith. After 30 years as a cancer surgeon, I have been exposed to the burdens of illness and death.

However, over the past five years as a member of Holy Family parish in Virginia Beach, I have had my faith brought into sharper focus and made more meaningful and I have also witnessed an inspiring outreach to the poor, sick and suffering. These and other blessings are a direct result of our pastor, Thomas Quinlan. Beneath the sometimes gruff exterior is an extraordinarily knowledgeable and compassionate individual who pursues all that is just and good with the energy of the Hound of Heaven.

I have never encountered anyone quite like him and I consider myself graced to have participated in this faith community under his guidance.

Paul F. Schellhammer, M.D.
Virginia Beach.

The Catholic Virginian

Serving the People of the Diocese of Richmond

LETTERS

Reader calls 'TQ' modern day prophet

Whether a position is in a church or in a secular field, it is always interesting to notice how the way one leaves a job is being characterized. Anyone familiar with the situation regarding TQ's (Father Thomas Quinlan) replacement at Holy Family Church in Virginia Beach knows this was no resignation, as your paper mentioned in the last issue. Why not be honest and say that he was fired by the bishop?

Like many others who know him far better, I have been personally affected and challenged by this modern day prophet. Although I live in Central Virginia, I always looked forward to my work trips in Tidewater, knowing that there was a good chance I would be available for one of TQ's adult education sessions. While most Catholic adult education is often watered down and at about an eighth grade level, his insight into scripture, and the history of the church, among other topics, offered me a far more scholarly and satisfying approach than I had ever received. But like other prophets, perhaps he was not recognized in his own diocese (in this case- and especially by a "visitor" from the Diocese of Arlington who chose to challenge TQ's understanding of Liturgy and procedures with his own narrow interpretation.

TQ will be missed by my entire family including our children and young adults, who looked forward to attending Liturgy more than at any other time and with any other celebrant. It was not unusual to have more than 20 members of my family at a time, some from other Christian churches, look forward to attendance at Sunday Mass at Holy Family, as some never did here or at other Catholic churches in the past. We never left Mass without speaking of his homily, his faithfulness to the Gospel, and his devotion to his responsibilities. His work for the people of Haiti is legendary.

Our family also knows TQ as the man who is humble enough to wear my dad's shoes. Shortly after he had celebrated my dad's funeral in 2000, which was right after he came to Holy Family, my mother noticed his shoes were pretty worn out. When she asked him what size he wore, she found out that it was the same size as my dad, and she had several pairs of his shoes still in his closet. So, she asked TQ if he would like to have my dad's shoes and he was glad to take them.

I am sorry for all the folks of Holy Family that your spiritual leader has been taken from you and will pray that you gain closure from this difficult experience. Your loss will also be experienced by your many visitors who came to know and appreciate your former pastor, instead of the vocal minority who felt it was best to write letters to a higher authority about him. Do not despair for long, for it is the ultimate authority who knows what TQ is really all about.

**Mike Warnalis
Bedford**

(Editor: Father Quinlan was not "fired" as pastor of Holy Family. The priest sent a copy of the letter from Bishop DiLorenzo to The Catholic Virginian in which the bishop recognized him for his many years of ministry to the diocese and said he was retiring him as pastor of Holy Family. Father Quinlan still retains faculties of the diocese and can celebrate the sacraments as he sees fit. He had asked Bishop DiLorenzo to stay on another year, but the bishop chose to retire him. Father Quinlan is 76. Every priest serves in a particular assignment at the discretion of the bishop who has ordinary jurisdiction of the diocese.)

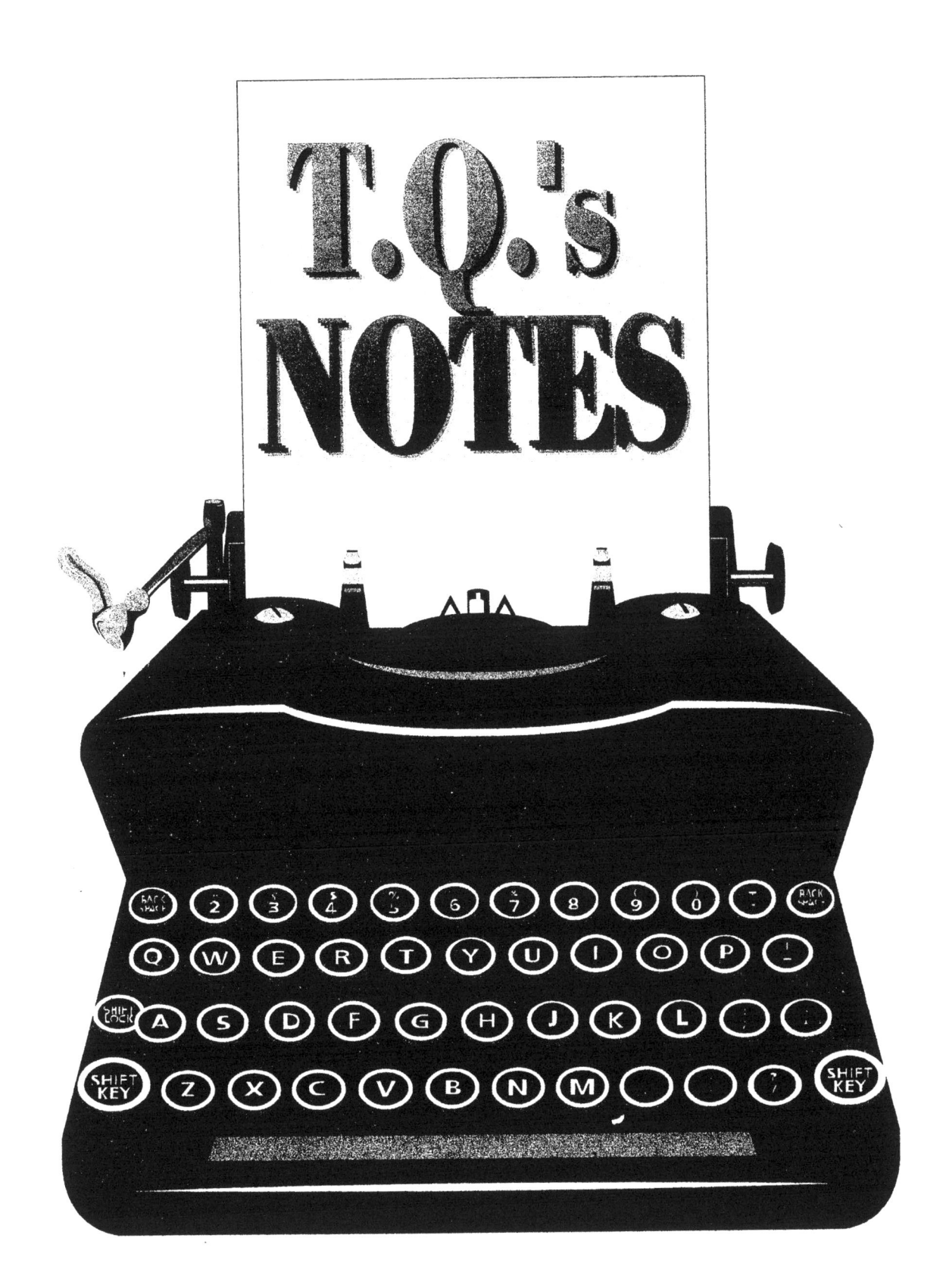

T.Q.'s NOTES

T.Q.'S NOTES

One of the tasks of a pastor is to keep his people prepared for a change in liturgy (on-going since Vatican II), in moral discernment (the moral<u>ities</u> of war and the new question of preemptive strikes) and the changing categories of theology in trying to make our Faith meaningful in a radically changed society. This is no easy task for any pastor and the people of God should be aware of the quickness, the adaptability, and the fruit of being prepared.

The hard-nosed Traditionalists try to make it into a heresy. The Fadist Fuzzie-Wuzzies pretend that they knew it all along. And the people in the middle wring their hands, and grunt or groan.

Hopefully none of the above constitutes the parish family of Holy Family. Not to mention the bare fact that one of the major purposes of having a pastor at all, is to have a person who is competent and fearless enough to prophesy over against his own people whom, we presuppose, he dearly loves. A pastor is not a state-hired clerk or cleric. A pastor does not play favorites. A pastor fears no parishioner despite his money, influence with the secular society, or even with the ordinary of any diocese. A BIG ORDER. Maybe that, more than celibacy, has decimated our ranks. (Not to mention the question of the ordination of women!!!) Today's 21st century pastor, while he leads the Liturgy, and is a sign of unity and Faith, more and more looks like a rabbi – one who knows the Scriptures <u>AND</u> Tradition inside out and interprets with and for the people of God.

One of the best examples of the seemingly new theology that a pastor is obligated to teach and implement is the question of <u>salvation</u>! Glibly, almost subconsciously, swallowed by all, it has to be rethought. Incidentally, the so-called new theology of SALVATION question has been around for centuries and there is the entire Franciscan School of Scotism that has never bought nor taught St. Thomas' opinion, which many consider to be Divine Teaching, including many of our own hierarchy. And of course the majority of our Protestant brothers and sisters. They believe that Christ suffered and died because of our sins, and especially the so-called ORIGINAL SIN. Not only does our reinterpretation of the Genesis Myth not allow that, but the conclusions that we formerly subscribed to as IMPLICATIONS OF THE GENESIS MYTH are now up for discussion, no small task for the pastor, the people (the thinking ones and the unthinking ones), the teenagers, and even some of the more precocious children. It's not only that we are not a sinful race, but that we went beyond Scripture and invented all kinds of assumptions and presumptions to try to explain the present condition of our race. It is tempting to push the question back and invent talking snakes, weak women, and seducible men to get the question out of the way. For the honest it won't work. We need new insights <u>built upon</u> the Franciscan teaching that Jesus would have come anyway, and that we do <u>not</u> need SALVATION, as hithertofore misinterpreted, as though we needed to be SAVED FROM – WHAT?? With a new understanding of the Bible, with a new world to frame it all in, and with a new age of honest Faith-filled reflections, we can build the New Theology. It will have subtle changes in prayer, the Mass, the Sacraments, but will change nothing substantially. And it will all become more real, more meaningful, and especially more honest.

The Breviary and Our Prayer Life

1. While private prayer can shift and change and have different centers, etc. because of our immediate needs – spiritual, emotional, psychological, even critical. But the prayer of the Church goes on forever. Public prayer is more fixed, more central, more theological, more ecological. It tries to sum up the sentiments of a gathered community in every age.

In the Western Church there are three facets of the one Divine Liturgy:

1. The celebration of Eucharist

2. The celebration of a Sacrament (sometimes without Eucharist)

3. The Singing or Recitation of the Divine Office (Breviary).

It is still amazing how many Catholics do not know this basic fact of prayer life.

The Breviary is the 150 psalms distributed throughout the monthly (lunar) cycle, together with Scripture Readings, antiphons, responsorials and songs. Its beauty is that it covers ALL. It is:

1. Theologically centered

2. Has ecological overtones that mean more today than when written

3. There is an ambit for every emotional moment in our lives

4. There are psalms for when we have sinned, when we are happy, when we are on pilgrimage, when we are sad

5. The psalms summarize all of creation: goats and hills, and mountains – creational sentiments as well as redemptive – includes animals, birds, trees, the sea, flowers, everything

Every Catholic should be identifiable by their owning of a Bible and a Breviary, not by rosaries, St. Christopher medals, plastic Jesuses on the dashboard, miraculous (?????) medals, scapulars (unless we really have joined and practice the rule of a Third Order), fundamentalistic cliché banners and bumper stickers, etc., etc.

If we all live to be 100 we will never plumb the depths of Scripture and the Mass and the Breviary and any Sacrament. Let's put our energies and prayer life on the essentials.

We are adults after all. Our prayer should manifest this to our parish family and to all nonbelievers. It is time to put away the trinkets of a child as St. Paul wrote!

November 19, 2000

T.Q. Notes - February 17-18, 2001:

1. WHAT WE BELIEVE - HOW WE LIVE

The integrity, the completedness, the fullness, the dynamism of all Christian Faith--particularly Catholic-Orthodox-- is the transcendental relationship, the intrinsic interconnectedness of Faith, Morality, and Liturgy. What you believe is exercised, put into practice by HOW you live (Morality) and celebrated (Liturgy) when we gather. There is not a catalog of dogmas out there. Then a list of rules in the next column. And finally a bunch of rubrics to sort of put it together.

LEX CREDENDI begets LEX AGENDI begets LEX ORANDI, i.e. what I believe as a disciple which comes form the four Gospel portraits of Jesus dictates to me how I am to live my life and the value system and FLOWS from knowledge of these teachings, and these are both put into sensuous, symbolic modes of celebrating, whether it be New Life, Suffering, Death, Resurrection, a Good Day, a Bad Day, an Aeon of Suffering, or a Moment of Death. Not to mention the fact that once we are really converted to Jesus and His New Way (of being a Jew) our entire value system is re-oriented, our attitudes attempt to imitate His more and more, and you celebrate these verities as a community whenever we assemble.

Examples: Once I am convinced Jesus founded a circle not a pyramid, I take on the ministry, attitude, way of life that reflects His more and more as I mature in the Faith. I wouldn't build a church that looks like a temple with the people separated from the priest, with high platforms, high altars, high platforms. The building of the worship area reflects this.

There are no private smoke-em-up rooms. There are no priest-and-me rooms, etc. The art and the music reflect a variegated but equal plane mode of worship. The priest, the nun, the married, the single, the hetero/homo-sexual, the wealthy, the homeless all perform the same rites. While there are special parts for the leader(s), there are reciprocal parts for each person.

Once I know that Communion is the sharing of the divine and human, and I also know that what I bring as necessary as what I receive at worship, the attitude (the morality) changes. People wouldn't be coming to Mass without food for the poor. It wouldn't make any sense. In fact one of the reasons for celebrating Mass is to keep reminding myself that I have got to keep bringing more, first, of myself in the Offering in order that I might receive more in the Giving, the Communion.

Once I understand God's universal forgiving I never look askance at anyone. I throw no stones, I examine myself and I am constantly in a state of humility because of the gifts I have so undeservedly been given, from God, from Jesus, from (Their) Church.

Half the acrimony, half the ignorance and most of the argumentation in today's Church would disappear once this interconnectedness becomes the norm in our parish.

T.Q. Notes - March 31-April, 2001 - also September 10, 2000:

THE MANY SOURCES OF OUR FAITH

A. The Church and Bible are coequal; No Church, no Bible - No Bible, no Church. **You can't have one without the other**. The Bible is necessary for:

Salvation

Revelation

Edification

Authentic Piety

B. The church as a *living*, breathing, changing, always correcting and correctable society, has **many** sources of Faith, among which the most important and the center of our Faith are:

The Bible. The Church wrote the New Testament, not vice versa. The Church has preserved both the New Testament and the Hebrew Scriptures (Old Testament). Since the people who read, pray over and apply the Bible have the same Faith as the people who wrote it, it becomes the Church's prerogative to **interpret** it. Catholics do not accept *the Bible alone* principle of 16th century Protestantism, and cannot therefore accept the **private** interpretation of the Scripture (which most intelligent Protestants no longer do either).

The Bible has been preserved for signing and reciting various parts each day in the official prayer book of the Catholic Church, the 150 psalms distributed throughout each week and month and feast day. This book is called the **Divine Office** or the **Breviary**.

In America, because we have a *I wanna quick Jesus* type of religion, people tend to read, interpret and pray over the book in a literal fashion. Also, in the USA we have groups like the Mormons, who literally believe that Joseph Smith found some hitherto fore unknown tablets of the Bible, called the Book of Mormon, in Palmyra, New York in 1830 and--not only that--they believe that God dropped down a pair of golden goggles from Heaven for him alone to interpret it!

The **other** sources of our faith are

Liturgy (Worship). How the people prayed tells us what the believed. **Lex credendi est lex orandi**. How they celebrated Mass, funerals, marriages, baptisms, Easter, in the Eastern and Western Churches in various centuries.

Catechesis. Catechisms = Study Books for those seeking to become Christina Catholics. Adult and children's books.

Fathers of the Church (Patrology). The people after the death of the Apostles (eye-witnesses of Jesus) who wrote and taught doctrine, morality, etc. For example, St. Augustine, St. Justin, St. Athanasius, St. Gregory Nyssa.

21 Ecumenical Councils. The gathering of the whole Church leadership of both the Eastern and Western Churches in union with the Bishop of Rome (vid. Pope). From Nicea, 325 C.E. to the Second Vatican Council, 1961-1965 C.E.

Ex-Cathedra (means *from the Chair of Peter, the first Bishop of Rome*). Statements of the Popes. More often than not, letters called encyclical (encompassing the whole world), rescripts, allocution stating Catholic doctrine or morals, but **not** from the official Chair. Therefore, important, but *not* absolute!
The Lives of the Saints. How thousands of Christians of exemplary life style lived out the Gospel message in each ear of Church History, in a zillion different professions and modalities of life, e.g., the Martyrs, the hermits, the monks and nuns, married people, bachelors, reformed prostitutes, geniuses, illiterate peasants, etc. For example: St. Anthony, the first hermit; St. Benedict; St. Thomas Aquinas; St. Margaret of Cortonna; St. Bridget of Sweden; St. Brigid of Kildaire, Ireland; St. Charles Borremeo; St. Martin de Porres; St. Kim Taegon; St. Peter Claver; St. Catherine of Siena.

T.Q. Notes - June 16-17, 2001:

THE BODY OF CHRIST

On the feast of the Body **and** Blood of Christ there are so many facets for reflection, it is difficult to be selective. First, this feast is a repeat of Holy Thursday. The reason for a repeat in the liturgical year should be obvious. It is such a central and Omni-encompassing mystery.

It did not develop, however, out of the best church-life circumstances. People had grown cold about its necessity and benefits and the People of God fell into a veritable puritanical praxis of their unworthiness even though Jesus had certainly initiated it for our sustenance. Then metaphysics took over theology, and even St. Thomas fell into a Host syndrome.

Originally at every Mass a roll or two was confected for the sick and the dying. This was taken back into the priest's house in case of
emergencies, etc. It was very secondary to the community meal, the
re-presentation of the sacrifice, etc. After a while the **unworthy** people stopped eating (and only **clergy** drank: and the Faith began a new rivulet, sc., taking the left-over rolls which had become hosts by then, and **staring at it**. This produced so-called Perpetual Adoration, Forty Hours, Benediction, and Corpus Christi processions. While praying in front of the Blessed Sacrament (Reserved Sacraments for episcopalians) is a good form of piety, the **ratio** (nature, essence, purpose) of this sacrament is that it be confected (made present) and eaten and drunk during a community meal of faith believers. This legacy of Jesus cannot be changed by relativistic pietists. Some of these later practices smack of primordial religious. Is Jesus more present when I look at His Presence (not Him) in a piece of glass? Isn't He truly and mysteriously present when He is in my fleshy mouth, esophagus, and stomach? Jesus said: "Take and Eat -- Take and Drink." He never even intimated: "Take and Stare !!!"

Perpetual Adoration is growing everywhere under a false **piety**. There is no doubt that there is much more real meaning to people who
celebrate Daily Mass and follow Jesus' mandate and effect the many effects of this Sacrament. Why go an stare at the Blessed Sacrament from 2:00 – 3:00 a.m. instead of getting up early and confecting this Sacrament at 7:30 a.m. Mass?

Not only that -- these practices have a tendency to create scandal among intelligent Protestants, many of whom (sad to say), lack Eucharist and only have **the Word**. But they have a right, with Bible in hand, to ask us "What are you doing?"

The Real Presence of Jesus in the Tabernacle is the source of food and health and light and life for those who cannot come. But the celebration of Daily Mass supercedes these practices **secundum omne**
excessum = according to every excess.

EAT AND DRINK. SELDOM STARE !

T.Q. Notes–May 12, 2002:

1. **Enjoy the Legends. Celebrate the Truth.**

While some people believe it to be merely semantics, scholars, scientists, theologians, and biblicists know that we have to have many a change in discussions, conversations, and dialog in our worship and spiritual lives. The arrival of the Feast of the Ascension (formerly Ascension Thursday) is an on-the-spot example. First and foremost, Jesus did not take off in a popcorn cloud up in the air, or rent a spacecraft in a sort of E.T. departure. While the people who wrote the Scriptures believed in a flat earth, with a solid sky above, and a deep hole underneath, we do not. Imagine telling a young child that this Sunday is the Feast of Jesus' Going-Up to Heaven. He would justifiably wince at his/her parents' ignorance of the planet and the galaxy that the planet is in, not to mention millions of other galaxies beyond.

Secondly, if this all took place in one day we still have to celebrate these staggering events, mysteries separately. Bible scholars do call them the *Exultation Mysteries* these days, and we should not be naïve about the celebrations of Easter, Ascension Day, and Pentecost.

Furthermore, it is incorrect to speak about the *Descent* of the Holy Spirit. Where did He/She descent from?

Another example which has completely lost its meaning is the *Assumption of the Blessed Virgin Mary*. If she has been assumed so are we all. What's so special about this day? Why not have a feast day dedicated to *Elijah-Going-Up-Into* (ugh)-*Heaven-in-a-Fiery-Chariot Day?*

And remember the olden times when we had the feast of *St. John the Baptist's Head on a Platter* (Sanctus Joannes in Disco), or people gathering in the Cathedral of Naples to witness the coagulation of blood in a vial on St. Januarius' feast day (September 19), which is also the feast of our Lady of LaSalette - the Virgin of the Alps weeping over our sins, which the right-wing fundamentalistic Catholics are now putting in Anti-Abortion Gardens.

These are fetishisms, not aspects of True Faith.

While we don't have to become literal, clinical, and least of all fanciful, we must celebrate the Truth. If there are legends around that make life a little more lightsome, romantic, or vista-vision fine. But let's not mix the two. If you lose something, don't be praying to St. Anthony (a Doctor of the Church, a Franciscan who actually lived). Besides no Catholic would pray **to** a saint anyway, but only in honor of one.

The demons of modern psychiatry are not much better, even though a good psychiatrist would tell you that they are all analogies. We're seeking the Truth, the Whole Truth, and nothing but the Truth.

Recent Changes to the Mass Include Bad Rubrics

In our church there is such an intimate and necessary connection between what we believe, how we act, and how we celebrate that we have to pay attention to any change which might move us back into a medieval church and other changes that might project us out of the church. The recent changes in the Mass are a perfect example. I have read the Commentary and it is totally unconvincing. Catholics have long, long, aeon-old memories that help us to evaluate change, for better or for worse. One of the memories we must call to mind is how Pope Adrian I suppressed all the beautiful local Missals (e..g., Canterbury in England, Bango in northern Ireland, etc.) and ordered that all western countries should use the Roman Missal ONLY. He did this to help Charlemagne and successors take over Europe!

1. Kneeling at certain parts of the Mass. What is more penitential? Kneeling, standing, or sitting? It depends. Kneeling does not show repentance any more than standing unless you are in a baronial, monarchical model. Some people like to scream when they are sorry for their past sins. Some like to tear their clothes. Some like to prostrate.

2. One point of the new rubrics is the only one I can find that is well taken. The Prayer of the Faithful is for GENERAL INTERCESSIONS, and not for lokum-yokum ones. Too many please for cancer and aids victims undermine the purpose. These should be prayers for the Universal Church and for the whole Human Race. I once had a parishioner at St. Vincent's, Newport News, who prayed during the 12:10 Daily Mass: "For my dentist's toe, we pray to the Lord." Give us all a break.

3. The priest should not leave the altar during the Kiss of Peace. This is the most important time for him to leave the altar to mingle with the People of God he claims to serve. Does Rome think that Jesus is going to escape form the Bread and Wine, His Body and Blood?

4. Eucharistic Ministers should approach the altar after the priest has taken Communion AND they are not allowed to pour wine into smaller chalices. There's the real rub. This presumption is that the priest is ABOVE the people, and God forbid, holier than the people, especially the carefully chose Eucharistic Ministers.

5. Bowing before taking the Bread and Cup. A bad rubric. It interferes with the flow of the Meal, of the Communion procession itself.

6. The poor Tridentine, Latin-Mass group! Standing is THE position for the reception of Communion. The Kiss of Peace is MANDATORY. What are Don't-Touch-Me people and Germ Whackos going to do??

The hidden agenda, as per usual, is the re-clericalization of the church together with artificial and necessary unity. If you believe in a monarchical church, you build a cathedral (theatre-style) with pews, keep out God's sunlight stained glass, and a big throne for the Massa' to sit on. If you believe that the People of God are THE CHURCH, then you build an aula (large banquet hall for all) because "form follows function," a principle of art, is more important in theology. How we build and celebrate tells us, even subconsciously, what we really believe. LEX ORANDI EST LEX CREDENDI, a principle of Faith, not a rubrical whim!

June 29, 2003

T.Q. Notes–June 14-15, 2003:

1. The Power of Prayer

Day after day in every situation and facet of life we hear the phrase "THE POWER OF PRAYER." If properly understood, it could have meaning. Of course we will never know the authentic power of prayer because we are not God.

The question often is surfaced more openly when people mistreat the meaning of the Prayer of PETITION. Some treat it as though it were their final ATM card in their relationships with God.

Furthermore the tendency to attribute to prayer a power all its own is very common in today's culture, both among Catholics with a childhood understanding of their Faith, and is rampant among all Fundamentalists.

Prayer is any thought, word, or action that makes us conscious of the presence of God in our lives. It is not necessarily formalized, articulated, or self-consciously thought.

It can be intuitive as well as planned.

Everyone should know that Prayer makes us:

1. Aware of God's presence in our lives and those around us, even of all creation.

2. That Prayer is a result of a personal Faith in a personal God.

3. That it does not change God's will but might help change ours, both passively and actively.

4. That it is the ultimate expression of our dependency upon God.

5. And that it is articulated in community often (especially during Liturgy) for the community's benefit.

It is summarized succinctly in the Preface of the Mass, Weekdays IV:

"YOU HAVE NO NEED OF OUR PRAISE,
YET OUR DESIRE TO THANK YOU IS ITSELF YOUR GIFT.
OUR PRAYER OF THANKSGIVING ADDS NOTHING TO YOUR GREATNESS,
BUT MAKES US GROW IN YOUR GRACE,
THROUGH JESUS CHRIST OUR LORD."

Prayer does nothing for God. It's all for US. Let's admit it and it will enhance our prayer life. Spontaneity is a desired quality of personal prayer, both during the Liturgy and in private prayer or devotion. When we pray each and every day with a spontaneity energized by the Holy Spirit, we become cognizant friends of God, not occasional drop-ins.

Pagans believe they can change their gods and goddesses' minds and wills. Mostly concerned with cereal (food) and fertility (children) concerns, they even sacrificed their own children (human sacrifices) to influence the gods, to change their wills, etc. Even the Jews fasted and prayed "to avert God's Punishment." We know we cannot and do not want to do that. We just want to tune in to God, have Him/Her with us, be one with Her/Him, show our naked dependence, and move on with God's/our lives.

T.Q. Notes–June 4-5, 2004:

The Catholic Church - Continuing Metamorphosis

One, of a thousand, benefits of being a member of the Catholic Church is that we have many sources for our Faith in the continuous and continuing Tradition, which means the power to RE-INTERRET the Gospel of Jesus and make certain accommodations as Saint Paul himself did in applying Jesus' teaching about divorce to the pagan Roman culture, popularly called the
Pauline Privilege.

If we were a Bible alone church we would be stuck in a box so tight we would be asphyxiated, as congregations are discovering. We have many sources of our Faith. We have the Bible at the center. We have twenty-one Ecumenical Councils (from 325 - 1965 C. E.). We have the Fathers and one Mother of the church (2nd to 9th centuries) of both Eastern and Western rites. We have two ex Cathedra teachings of the Bishop of Rome (rather secondary in nature and importance). And we have the Lives of the Saints, forever renewing the Church in every culture from every walk of life in every eon of Church history, many of them prophesying against our own Church and its legalisms, rubricisms, power-grabbing and mirroring-the-Secular-Society institutionalisms.

The Church is like a caterpillar. It looks asleep and the egotists think they are hiding, but a new spring blows in and a butterfly emerges, free as an eagle, but much more beautiful. The Church is like a snake (not the talking snake of the Genesis Myth, negatively pictured) but the snake, again when spring or a new spring in our case, draws nigh, the snake slithers out of the old skin and continues to crawl through the universe, gleaming in the sunlight of a virtual rebirth.

You can't have a hang-up and be Catholic. There are a million cocoons and a trillion snake skins, from which the Church can extricate itself at any moment, until the last day of history, or the end of time as we used to call it. And when you believe this, and know it, you will be as free as the Saints, especially if you are called upon to live out your Catholic Faith in the most decadent times, in the darkest hour, etc.

We are Catholic! Free as a Bird! Light as a Feather! Fearless as a Tiger! Plenipotential in every facet of life!

T. Q. NOTES

"'Twas the night before Christmas" - oops, wrong poem. "'Twas a sad day in Confederate City" - May 24, 2004, the day of the installation of the 12th bishop of Richmond, Virginia!!

1. The venue was horrendous. Our "beautiful" cathedral, nostalgized by the editor of "The Catholic Virginian" is the most unsuitable site in the state. Over thirty years ago when Carroll T. Dozier, pastor of Christ the King, Norfolk, was ordained <u>and</u> installed in the small midland diocese of Memphis, Tennessee, it was celebrated in the Mid-South coliseum with 15,000 present on a most frigid day. About 900 of our 215,000 people were present May 24. The People of God were cut out. The Richmond Coliseum is near by.

2. The music was so triumphant I thought we were in the so-called "National(?) Cathedral, feeling like I was awaiting the arrival of the Monarch-sanctioned Archbishop of Canterbury. No African-American drums or voices, no Korean or Filipino or Hispanic guitars and other instruments. The tri-lingual intercessions were a farce. Who speaks Latin in Richmond? Who in this diocese can pass a 9th grade Latin exam? A bunch of WASP hymns and anthems blasted out on the 55-rank pipe organ by a musicologist who plays <u>to</u> himself and <u>for</u> the dead!

3. For the first time in memory there were no LAY extraordinary ministers of the Eucharist distributing the Body and Blood of Christ. The sea of white vested clerics (deacons and priests) "grabbed" everything with a sort of "it's our Church" possessiveness. A GIRMness pervaded all.

4. There was no real representation of Tidewater parishes where more than half the Catholics live. The bishop was greeted by three monsignors from the city of Richmond which is NOT the center of the diocese by any standard. Tidewater, Roanoke, Appalachia, and Bristol, Virginia-Tennessee might as well have stayed home and had picnics in any one of our state parks.

5. And the procession itself was counter-ecclesial, red and magenta pom-pom wearers assembling in the episcopal palace, separated from the <u>lower</u> clergy, and the Protestants and Anglicans separated from both.

6. And after the great foot-washin' pericope of the Fourth Gospel, we had a homily about the implementing of our vision by the use of a manual, already long forgotten, that caused a wave of tittering among the priests, and a hundred whispered "what book is he talking about?" not to mention, one old presbyter muttering: " Is Gorbachev here? Communists use manuals, not Catholics."

7. And finally, the lack of the full presence of our former <u>female</u> chancellor who was given "woman's work," inviting us to the reception. On the other, right, hand, of our new Ordinary, we experienced the full <u>male</u> presence of Bishop Joseph A. Gallante, the Eucharist-refusing, conscience-judging new bishop of Camden, New Jersey.

And all this counter-personal to a broad, tall, vibrant, ever-embracing, smiling <u>paesan</u>!

"'Twas a sad, sad day in Richmond."

Christmas ~ Epiphany 2004/2005

January 6, 2005

Dear Friends:

I know you all think you have heard the latest news. But you haven'! The news of the death of the Pope, the tapping on the forehead three times with the silver hammer by the Dean of the Cardinals to make sure he is dead, stone daid! And then the deadlocked conclave - for six months. Most cardinals have lost thirty-five or more pounds. It has so frustrated one cardinal that he snuck into the Sistine Chapel at night and smashed the papal Ballot Stove to pieces with an axe. No more WHITE SMOKE OVER THE VATICAN. No more smoke (and mirrors)???? Hmm. This so upset the others they decided that they just had to do something unheard of – and they did!!! Cardinal Rigali, a most Vaticanese stalwart, offered to purchase personal computers for the 1,000,000,000 plus Catholics on the planet, but retracted when a cardinal from Africa sneered: "You might need that money to pay off sacerdotal sexually abused victims".

They decided that since their "system" wasn't working, they would use the approach of another system, that of the Dalai Lama. So they surreptitiously selected a naive cardinal from Vietnam and sent him to Bethlehem Pennsylvania, United States of America to see if he couldn't find another star and some bartenders (their version of contemporary shepherds) to discern the next Chosen One. Since he had never been in the U. S, when he arrived in Bethlehem, feeling starved after a long air flight and a thumbed ride in a Pole's pick-up truck, he jumped out and entered the first eatery he could find – CZELUSNIAK'S STABLE. Because of the language barrier the bartender, a devout Ruthenian Catholic, kept sliding martini after martini down the bar, together with several Kielbasa sandwiches. The Vietnamese cardinal thought it was bottled water, all the while wondering why there was always an olive floating on top. "Maybe it's an American custom", he said to himself. After an hour or so he began to feel disoriented, indeed very high, and the shaggy bartender took on the appearance of a shepherd – not to mention when he looked out the window he could see a mammoth star shining in the sky over beyond some high building (not realizing that it was from the Chamber of Commerce creche in the middle of the town). "THIS IS IT", he shouted to the now empty bar. He grabbed a small candelabra from the bar and walked down Nativity Lane to see what he could see. As he passed a stoop of an apartment building the candle light settled on a rather handsome pubescent, smoking a cigarette. Without a word of conversation, he drew out ten one-hundred dollar bills from his pocket (that had been placed there by the carmelengo as he left Rome), and offered it to him. He took the, stood up, and followed the cardinal to the airport.

He, at fifteen (another boy Pope, ho-hum), was ordained a deacon, a presbyter and a bishop all at one Mass in the Sistine chapel (shades of St. Ambrose) and then paraded out, minus miter, to be installed in St. Peter's Square. The two million people packed into the square and its environs were hysterically happy: the cardinals sullen.

The whole world expected a regent-cardinal to be appointed. But as there was no communique from the Pope's spokeslady (the only appointment in his first week), a six-foot two blonde from Denmark with a mermaid aura. Apprehension smoldered in every Curial office. One old Polish cardinal was heard to mutter; "He must be in the papal playroom, examining the two million dollars of toys sent by the evil American corporations." Not to be fooled, Dylan I (that's his name) took only one item out of the humongous pile - a white American tricycle!!

His first votive Mass was celebrated in St. John Lateran's (the Pope's real parish church - he never again celebrated in St. Peter's, only in the Square) at the end of his first month. And it was a Liturgy to remove from the canonization process Pio Non, Pius XII and Anne Catherine Emmerich. There were only two shocks during this Mass. At the Kiss of Peace he jumped onto his papal white tricycle and zipped all over the basilica shaking hands with hundreds of people, even in the back corners and narthex. Those ancient walls almost tumbled, so wild was the jubilation of the People of God. At the end of the Mass he went to the pulpit and announced the suppression of GIRM (General Instruction for the Roman Missal). His tricycle became the symbol of this welcomed action.

Then his reign really began

His first encyclical appeared:

DE VOLUPTATIBUS LECTI MARITALIS DEODATIS. This pronouncement "Concerning the God-designed Pleasures of the Marriage Bed" abrogated the paragraph (only) in Paul VI's HUMANAE VITAE about the necessity of every act of intercourse being open to new life, but reaffirmed and praised the work. He mocked St. Thomas' innocent biologism about the infusion of a human soul of a man and a woman in the fifth and seventh month (respectively) after conception. He enunciated an ancient option: henceforward all sexual ethics would be based on the order of reason and not simply on the order of nature. This first encyclical was occasioned by his sneaking off, as he often did, to have a diet-lemon Coke and chew imported strawberry-flavored licorice "ropes" at a sidewalk cafe near St. Anne's Gate. Sitting down in an iron chair he realized he was sitting next to a Ukrainian priest with a beard that almost touched the street. Unrecognized in his designer shorts (a gift from Macy's) and T-shirt reading "I Love Mother Earth", the conversation turned into the priest's life story (almost biblical) He had had four wives, one dying at 24, one at 31, the third at 37, and the last at 42, each leaving him with three sons. His nickname was Isaac. He reminisced dramatically about the delights of his married life, about the trysts in log cabins and snow banks, etc. And how, now, on Saturday nights, he would gather himself alone in his Curial apartment, have a few Vodkas, and watch the movie "Doctor Zhivago", weeping tears of joy and thanksgiving, his preparation for Sunday morning Liturgy at the church of Saints Nereus and Achilles. (His real name was Father Igor Petripolitavkov!)

One day, sitting in a hidden cove in the Vatican Library, he opened his school backpack emblazoned with its "Our Lady of Czestochowa Parish School", and pulled out a magenta-colored legal pad (a gift from Staples) and rushed off a memo, excuse me, Rescript: DONUM NON MANDATUM CELIBATUS, "The Gift not the Mandate of Celibacy". In it he extolled the charism of a chaste celibate life as a signpost to eternal life and service to the community, but pointing out absence of any connection of this freely accepted gift with the Orders of bishop, presbyter, and deacon in the Catholic or Orthodox churches, documenting the errors of the Council of Elvira in 305 C. E.

About two months later, pedaling through throngs of Australian pilgrims in one of those long corridors on his tricycle with his parochial school backpack in the basket, he took a quick right turn into one of the offices, and without saying a word, dropped a large bundle of magenta-colored legal sheets on the desk of a fastidiously dressed female monsignor. It turned out that it was his second encyclical.

Entitled AD AEFDIFICIANDUM ORDINEM PRESBYTERORUM ET NOVUM ORDINEM PRESBYTER-A-RUM, i. e. "The Building Up of the Order of Presbyters (male) and The New Order of Presbyters (female)". In this document he affirmed the equality of the genders, their differences, and laid bare the silliness of antiquated traditions, purporting some kind of transcendental relationship between the "Persona Christi" and penises and testicles, etc. Because of its importance worldwide, the ordination of a thousand priests, five-hundred male and five-hundred female, would take place in Tienanmen Square in China on Holy Thursday, April 13, 2006 at High Noon. (Because of the imagined distances of this humongous plaza he reveled in the possibilities of using a skateboard instead of his beloved tricycle!)

Dylan's third encyclical followed within three months. VERSUS RESTAURANDA PRINCIPIA SODALITATIS ET CONSENSUS NOVI TESTAMENTI, "Toward Restoring the Principles of Collegiality and Consensus from the New Testament", it abolished the College of Cardinals, the offices of archbishop and archabbot, Mother General, Protonotaary Apostolics, Archmandrites, Monsignori, and on and on. It emphasized a new way of exercising the primacy of the bishop of Rome, the leadership roles of bishops (overseers), presbyters, and especially deacons and deaconesses (whose role in the community had been hierarchized) The 1,000,000,000 plus Catholics could vote from Beijing to Butte, Montana, on papal- white voting machines, paid for by the melting down of the solid gold triptych of the Cathedral of Seville. All members of the fourteen-branched Orthodox communities were also invited to join in – all they had to do was produce a Baptismal-Confirmation certificate.

The next day a sudden Rescript also appeared: <u>INCACERATIO OMNIUM EPISCOPORUM INVOLUTI CUM ABUSU SEXUALE INNOCENTIUM</u> (The Imprisonment of All Bishops Involved with the Sexual Abuse of the Innocents"). Not only were they to be defrocked publicly in their own cathedrals by the various Papal Emissaries, but they were to be flown to Rome under Swiss Guard vigilance, and sent to the Sacred Penitentiary where they were to fast for seven years and seven Lents, and they were to wear over their prison jump-suits emblems reading <u>FURCIFERES</u>, i. e., Jailbirds.

And just when the Joy, Hope, and Openess, reminiscent of the post-Conciliar era was romping along, Pope Dylan died of a cerebral hemorrhage. And the whole Catholic world cried out,. In imitation of its Jewish ancestors: "WHERE IS GOD WHEN WE NEED HER/HIM????

T. Q.

OUCH...

SHLESINGER, ARKWRIGHT, GARVEY & DINSMORE

PATENT TRADEMARK & COPYRIGHT LAW

CRYSTAL PLAZA OFFICE BUILDING
2001 JEFFERSON DAVIS HIGHWAY
ARLINGTON, VIRGINIA 22202

B. EDWARD SHLESINGER, JR.
GEORGE A. ARKWRIGHT
GEORGE A. GARVEY
JACK Y. DINSMORE

HAROLD H. DUTTON, JR.
JOHN F. HOFFMAN
REG. PATENT AGENTS

B. EDWARD SHLESINGER
PHILIP K. FITZSIMMONS
BERNARD F. GARVEY (1891-1967)
COUNSEL

GEORGE A. TEW
REG. PATENT ATTORNEY

AREA CODE: 703
521-1500
CABLE: SHLES

May 24, 1972

Reverend Thomas J. Quinlan
Pastor, Good Shepherd Church
3321 Wessynton Way
Alexandria, Virginia

Re: Christ and His Church As
It Relates To Good Shepherd
Parish

Dear Reverend Father Quinlan:

This letter will confirm our conference on May 15, 1972, at the rectory. In conjunction therewith this letter brings current the various episodes and events which have caused me to take a position adverse to your pastorate and in effect, necessitates my making every effort to seek your removal as pastor in order that the true Doctrine of the Catholic Church be taught from Good Shepherd Parish. I can no longer sit idly by hoping for a change for the better. I see great harm being done to the followers at Good Shepherd with many being blindly lead astray with your charisma and authoritativeness into believing what you say is the authentic teaching of the Church.

You have a large following who are ready and willing to accept your heretical ideas and views even to the extent that they might turn away from the Pope and his teachings and those teachings of the Bishops when acting in concert. Your method of attack is insidious and subtle and preys on the lack of knowledge of most of the Faithful of Good Shepherd. They follow blindly like lambs to the slaughter.

Your attack is direct and against Dogma and wages war against Christ and His Church. It generally follows the course of Modernism (Item #1) condemned by the Holy Office by "Lamentabile" published July 3, 1907, and by Pope Pius X on September 8, 1907, in his encyclical "Pascendi Dominici Gregis".

In addition to the heresy preached, you have also totally disregarded and swept aside many of the strictly prescribed Rubrics. And further, you, by indirection and even openly, criticized Magesterium of the Church and downgraded to the extent to ridicule many aspects of reverence, piety so important to the Church even with regard to well known personal revelations "which though not

Reverand Thomas J. Quinlan
May 24, 1972
Page 2

required to be believed"; nevertheless, are encouraged and promoted by the Church as doing honor to God, His Mother and the Saints. e. g. Fatima (Item #2).

In regard to heresy, you have done the following:

1. Ridiculed the Profession of Faith (Creed) and in many instances omitted it completely from Saturday evening and Sunday Mass.

2. Declared from the pulpit at Holy Thursday Mass, that the washing or the feet is "the greatest Sacrament". It is of course not even one of the Seven Sacraments. True, the word sacrament in the broad sense of the word and in the early Church applies to many things such as Christ and the Church because they are sacred signs and mysteries; nevertheless, the Church today uses Sacrament to give special meaning to the Seven Main Rights of Christian worship.

3. Stated in the evening Mass of May 13, 1972, that "Mary, the Mother of God, that is the Mother of Jesus, cannot be taken literally". The Church clearly proclaims that Mary is the Mother of God and the Mother of Jesus and it can only be taken literally. That Mary was not the Mother of the first and third persons of the Trinity does not negate her being the Mother of God in a literal sense. It can only be so. If it is otherwise, then it denies that Christ is God. (Item #3, page 84 and Item #4, page 92 from the Constitution of the Church signed by Pope Paul IV, November 21, 1964).

4. Stated at the evening Mass of May 13, 1972, that the teaching of the Immaculate Conception was "not that dogmatic". However, this is declared doctrine just as is the Assumption (Item #5).

5. Stated at the evening Mass of May 13, 1972, that "a popular notion" that Mary is Dispensatrix and Mediatrix of all Graces is not a teaching "of the Church". But in truth, this is a teaching of the Church (Items #5 and #6).

6. Further, at the same Mass, you stated that asking Mary or the Saints "for Bon Bons - that's crazy when you have Christ to ask directly". But this is also contrary to the teaching of the Church (Item #6 and #7) which deal with invocation of Mary and the Saints. (Defined by the Counsil of Trent).

Reverand Thomas J. Quinlan
May 24, 1972
Page 3

7. Further, on several occasions from the pulpit, you have spoken blasphemously of indulgences as being ridiculous. But the Doctrin of Indulgence was defined by the Council of Trent, Pope Saint Pius V in 1567. (Item #8). Now "blasphemy" should be here defined. (Item #9).

8. At least on one occasion at Mass, and to me personally in our conference, you disclaimed a belief in angels. As to the devil, you stated "frankly, I don't believe in him". This is also contrary to the Doctrine of the Church as taught by Fourth Lateran Council in 1215 and the Constitution of the Church. (Item #10-13).

The above items deal specifically with Doctrine but the following items also deal generally with failure to obey ecclesiastical authority as to Rubrics and comments made generally touching on the Doctrine and as a priest you are bound by vow of obedience to your Bishop but in this you fail:

1. From the pulpit you stated in the last weekend in April, relative to the hierarchy, "many evil men" are in the Church "but the most evil are Bishops".

2. You permitted our Cantor, Mr. Keith Ramey, on May 6, 1972, to speak from the pulpit before the entrance hymm, error which you did not correct although you were present. Mr. Ramey stated that we the people in conjunction with the priest bring Christ down on the altar and that the priest cannot do it without our assistance. This is clear heresy as we who are true Catholics know that only the priest can bring about the Transubstantiation.

3. At a week day evening Mass during Lent, you stated of the Rosary, "silly repetitious nonsense" and "the lowest form of prayer".

4. On numerous occasions from the pulpit you have ridiculed the Council of Trent and when confronted at our conference on May 15, 1972, when I said there were many good things that came from the Council, you said "yes, but 90% was bad". But, at Trent was defined among other things:

    a) Indulgences
    b) Two Sources of Revelation
    c) Original Sin
    d) Grace

Reverand Thomas J. Quinlan
May 24, 1972
Page 4

      e) Free Will
      f) That there are only Seven Sacraments
      g) The Transubstantiation and the Christ is Whole and entire under both species
      h) Mass is a true sacrifice
      i) That penance in order to be valid must be by an ordained priest having jurisdiction.

As a matter of fact, Vatican II is only a continuation of Trent.

5. You have administered, during Lent particularly and permitted your assistants to administer, the Eucharist in the hand to anyone who would accept it although in Bishop Russell's pastoral letter to all his priests sent out during Holy Week, the Bishop specifically states "the prohibition of the Church" "of Holy Communion received in the hand" is an "illegitimate departure" [transposition of the wording mine]. (Item 14, quoted from the Wonderer of May 4, 1972).

6. You <u>never</u>, as required by the Rubrics, make the sign of the <u>Cross</u> at the Gospel on the book, forehead, lips and heart.

7. You <u>never</u> elevate the Host as required with the fingers of both hands, but instead elevated it on the paten.

8. You <u>never</u>, as required, genuflect after each elevation.

9. You <u>never</u> recite the words of introductory as set out in the <u>missal</u> exactly as set out before the Our Father.

10. You <u>always</u> change the words introductory to "the kiss of peace".

11. You <u>frequently</u> pass the Blessed Sacrament in the tabernacle before and after Mass and during Mass, when you are not officiating without genuflecting.

12. You had no crucifix at all on the altar or centrally disposed with regard thereto on Holy Saturday when the main crucifix was covered completely and the small altar crucifix removed. Incidentally, the main crucifix is still covered and has been from the Holy Week services until now.

Reverand Thomas J. Quinlan
May 24, 1972
Page 5

13. You have frequently left our Church barren of any statues of Our Lord, Saint Joseph or the Good Shepherd (the only ones we have had) and the only images in our sanctuary presently are those of Our Lady and a crucifix approximately 8 inches high which rests on the altar. (Items #15-17)

14. You stated at Christmas time that the crib was an archaic symbol which "we as up to date Christians" should eliminate. At Christmas time there were no statues in the sanctuary at all, having been replaced with Christmas trees, the crib being relegated to the vestibule.

15. You frequently say at the Consecration, rather than the prescribed words, "this is My Body which shall be broken for you". I said in our conference that these words could not be found in the New Testament and I asked you to show me. But you failed, and said they were in some translation that you could not find but could if you looked long enough. I then pointed out that Christ's crucifixion was unique as no bone was broken as prophesied by the prophets before the coming of Christ. Then you said "well his body was broken and bruised" to which I agreed that his flesh was broken but that this was not the significance of these words. I had anticipated your arguing the point that Christ meant that he was about to break the bread at the Last Supper, but you never mentioned this so that I can only conclude that you never thought of this as a possibility and that you failed to use the proper wording as set out by the Rubrics either because of carelessness or because you desire them to detract from the truth of the sacrifice before us.

16. You permitted the Mass to be celebrated with vessels not lined with gold or silver as required. You frequently use an earthenware chalice and on Holy Thursday and Holy Saturday many such earthenware chalices were used. True, in the early days of the Church this was common, but Rubrics require the vessel to be of a precious metal today.

There are many hard working and industrious souls in our parish doing what they believe is right. I can overlook the banners covering the crucifix, the butterflies from the ceiling, the flickering and rotating lights, the film strips and slides during the Euchristic services, rock and chamber music, the ballons, fire crackers, sparklers, the cantor dressed in an alb and other lectors and commentators dressed in priestly robes who have no right to wear them, and the

Reverand Thomas J. Quinlan
May 24, 1972
Page 6

Deacon who is allowed to distribute communion on Sunday wearing dungarees, and many other minor matters, but I cannot disregard the open and vicious attack which you are making on Holy Mother the Church.

I shall continue to report variances from the Truth until either you conform or are removed or until our parish no longer has the sacrifice of the Mass, at which time I must depart. I ask our Lord to deliver us from this peril.

Very respectfully yours,

B. Edward Shlesinger, Jr

BESjr/jr

Enclosures

cc: Bishop John J. Russell
    Auxillary Bishop Walter Sullivan
    Monsignor T. T. Scannell
    Monsignor Richard Burke
    Monsignor J. D. McClunn
    Membership of Good Shepherd Council

June 9, 1972

Reverend John J. Russell
Bishop of Richmond
807 Cathedral Place
Richmond, VA 22320

Re: Reverend Thomas J. Quinlan
Pastor of Good Shepherd Church
Mount Vernon, VA

Dear Bishop Russell:

I am writing to you, as the Shepherd and Leader of the Diocese of Richmond, partially in response to a letter I have seen that was sent to you (and several other Priests of the Diocese) concerning Father Quinlan by Mr. B. Edward Shlesinger, Jr. My main purpose in writing, however, is to affirm my positive support of Father Quinlan and his ministry at Good Shepherd Community. As one who has known Father Quinlan since his first assignment in this Diocese at Blessed Sacrament Parish, Alexandria, I have only the highest respect and praise for him, both as a Priest and as a truly warm, human Person.

I am a registered member of Good Shepherd Parish, even though I live outside its boundaries and must travel considerable distance in order to join in celebrating Mass there. Part of my reason for joining Good Shepherd Community is that I believe that what Father Quinlan is doing there is in line with the teachings of the Post-Vatican II Catholic Church. I also firmly believe that Father Quinlan is doing a better job of true Catholic Pastoral Ministry than any other Pastor or Priest in the Northern Virginia area.

The Parish of the Good Shepherd is the only Community in the Northern Virginia area that has a completely functioning and open Parish Council. This Council makes the decisions and directs which courses of action the Parish will follow in all areas of Religious Development.

The Community of Good Shepherd has beautiful, self-renewing Liturgies in which the greatest majority of people I have ever seen really participate in celebrating. I have never seen so many persons join in the partaking of the Eucharist.

It is my belief that what is done by Father Quinlan in initiating positive ideas and thoughts at Good Shepherd Parish is in line with the thinking of the majority of the Community. The Parish Council, which is elected by all members of the church, has completely endorsed Father Quinlan's ministry at Good Shepherd.

In regards to Mr. Shlesinger's letter to Father Quinlan dated May 24, 1972, I feel compelled to make several remarks. I feel the most interesting statement made by Mr. Shlesinger is in the last paragraph of his letter, in which he states, "Until either you conform or are removed or until our parish no longer has the Sacrifice of the Mass, at which time I must depart, I ask our Lord to deliver us from this peril." I must question to you the basic Christian attitudes and common sense of Mr. Shlesinger in making such a statement. How can he as a faithful Catholic believer in the Life of Christ, even remotely suggest the possibility of no Celebration of Mass?

I do not intend to answer Mr. Shlesinger's letter point by point, as I feel that would be nothing more than an exercise in the futility of one man's opinion against another. I would like to make one last comment. Does Mr. Shlesinger go to Mass to remove Father Quinlan as Pastor of Good Shepherd Community, or does he go there in the spirit of joy to celebrate the sacred mysteries of the Mass?

I ask these questions to you as the Leader and Shepherd of God's Community in the Diocese of Richmond. I would be most interested in hearing from you, with any comments you have. I am not trying to be vindictive toward Mr. Shlesinger; but I do not believe that it is right or justifiable for any one person to level some of the charges he has made against Father Quinlan

-3-

in his letter of May 24, 1972.

If what Mr. Shlesinger says is really true, he should assemble a majority of Good Shepherd parishioners, who are against Father Quinlan's actions, and solid proof of his accusations. If he can assemble such a majority, I will endorse his actions in attempting to remove Father Quinlan as Pastor of Good Shepherd.

I don't believe Mr. Shlesinger's thoughts are those of the followers of Good Shepherd Church. I believe the people of this community endorse and Love Father Quinlan, and realize just how much they need him as their Pastor.

I thank you for your time and attention to this letter and hope the Spirit of Christ directs any action you take in response to Mr. Shlesinger's letter.

Respectfully yours,

Carl F. Greenwald
2625 N. Van Dorn Street #11
Alexandria, VA 22302

cc: Auxillary Bishop Walter Sullivan
    Monsignor T. T. Scannell
    Monsignor J. D. Mc Clunn
    Mr. B. Edward Shlesinger Jr.
    Reverend Thomas J. Quinlan
    Msgr. Richard Burke

THE ADMINISTRATOR OF NATIONAL BANKS
WASHINGTON

May 25, 1972

The Most Reverend
John J. Russell, D.D.
807 Cathedral Place
Richmond, Virginia 23220

Dear Bishop Russell:

I know you receive letters from time to time in which I and other members of parishes in your diocese write to lodge complaints or register objections to rulings and practices with which we disagree.

I sometimes wonder, however, how many of us take the time to write you when we agree with the general direction which parish and diocesan affairs are taking. Probably far too few so I am taking a few moments to give you my view of progress in Good Shepherd Parish, Alexandria, Virginia.

Since Father Thomas Quinlan became our Pastor in the summer of 1971, progress has been remarkable. There have been some growing pains. There were, and still are, some who objected to some of the changes, but the growth in our community has been broad and deep. The renewal initiated by Vatican II has been made meaningful to us. We participate in the liturgy as never before. Much of this participation is by some who, at the outset, strenuously opposed change.

The organization we established is bringing more parishioners into active participation in parish affairs. More than that, it is working. For the first time, priorities have been established which reflect the wishes of the majority of our community. Each parish committee is working to determine the community will in the area in which it functions. This has been painful for some in one or two areas, but I find an overwhelming number of the people with whom I discuss these matters pleased that the wishes of the majority of our community are being followed.

All of this is due principally to Father Quinlan. Without his faith, understanding, and guidance this progress would not have been made nor would there be the continuing growth which I see. As the Good Shepherd community continues to grow, there will be fewer and fewer who complain, although, among the holdouts, there will be some whose objections are probably the most strenuous. There will be far more who open their minds and learn to make the Gospel more and more a part of their daily lives.

It was a blessed day for Good Shepherd Parish the day you made the decision to assign Father Quinlan as our Pastor.

Most sincerely yours,

W. A. Howland, Jr.
Administrative Assistant to the
Comptroller of the Currency

Mr. & Mrs. Boyce L. Campbell, Jr.
8419 Mt. Vernon Hwy
Alexandria, Va. 22309

24 August 1972

The Most Reverend John J. Russell STD
Bishop of Richmond
800 Cathedral Place
Richmond, Va. 23220

Dear Bishop Russell,

Please accept this letter as one of joy. Joy because you sent to our parish, Good Shepherd, Alexandria, Va., Father Thomas Quinlan, to lead us in the announcement of the Good News. Father Quinlan is constantly serving this parish in the best manner he knows and because of this service our Christian lives have been greatly enriched which, of course, includes above all other reasons, bringing us closer to Christ.

His programs to progressively carry-out changes to this parish have been totally acceptable to me. I personally hope that his duties will continue to lead Good Shepherd to a new dialogue with what I believe are the concepts of the present-day church.

It is our desire and I hope it is also yours that Father Quinlan's pastoral services to Good Shepherd continue well into the future; For in him, there is a glimmer of hope of long overdue revitalization in the religious life of this parish.

Sincerely yours

Boyce L. Campbell Jr
& Family

His Eminence Joseph Cardinal Ratzinger
Prefect, Congregation of the Faith
11 PIAZZO Del. S.
UFFIZIO
Rome, Italy 300193

Dear Cardinal Ratzinger,

Regretfully I must report to you one of the most traumatic events of my life, and of my family's.

On October 24, 1991 my father died at the Bayside of Poquoson Convalescent Center. The death certificate states he died at 7:AM The Center called me, and I arrived there within 20 minutes. I immediately asked that a priest be called. The Center has a list of Chaplains that serve the facility. Father James Quinlan was therefore called. He arrived within 15 to 20 minutes after being phoned. He walked into the room wearing a light beige suit and brown shoes. He introduced himself, walked to the bed, and said a very short prayer, followed by the Our Father. He then stated--"Well that's it!". I said, Father we are Traditional Catholics, and I want my father anointed and the last rites administered. Throwing his arm in the air, he stated--"We don't do that anymore, Its Prohibited!". "You are a dying breed-Thank God!". I was so astonished and offended I could not speak. At this time of grief, I was not in the frame of mind to argue with him. He then said, "How Long was he here?". My husband, who was there during this entire event and witnessed what was said, then replied, one month. "I never saw him", Father Quinlan replied. "I don't come here often, my ministers take care of this".

This is the priest (title not deserved) who writes editorials in the Poquoson Post (local paper) that even our Baptist and Methodist brothers have answered in editorial response, exposing him for his errors in Faith. His only interests in this community are Social Issues and the Recycling Program.

I must explain that when I moved here 2 1/2 years ago, I heard of Fr. Quinlan's reputation. My husband and I decided we must find another church, that at least would not be offensive. After Church Shopping in surrounding area for a number of weeks, and being unable to find a Catholic Church, we decided to join the Chapel at Langley Air Force Base. Since my husband is stationed at Langley AFB as a Department of Defense employee, we were eligible to join the Chapel. We do not attend any services in Poquoson. Fr. Quinlan's reputation is well known all over the area, and he is considered a disgrace to the Catholic Community.

2

    We took my father to Maryland for burial. I related the incident to the Pastor of our home parish. He immediately said--"This is Heresy!'. "You must report this to the Bishop immediately, It is your Catholic duty".

    I told him the Bishop of Virginia was Walter J. Sullivan, who would completely ignore this, because many many reports of Heresy have been taken to him about Fr. Quinlan for 15 years and there were no results. He was promoted, and his influence advanced.

    Bishop Walter J. Sullivan has given the project of building a church here in Poquoson to Fr. Quinlan. Fr. Quinlan then stated to the Poquoson Post (paper) "I told the architect if this Worship Center even resembles a church I will make him tear it down".

    After my father's funeral I began to research this matter. I found in my book--Fundamentals of Catholicism, Kenneth Baker, S.J. Volume 3 page 314-315.....The Sacrament may not be administered to one who is certainly dead. Often however, there is doubt about whether a person is dead or not. When there is doubt the priest may anoint the person conditionally. By this is meant that the priest says, before administering the sacrament, "If you are alive"....or "If you are capable of receiving the sacrament"......Evidence points to the probability that the soul does not leave the body immediately when the signs of life cease. Thus one can anoint an <u>apparently dead person for a number of hours</u> afterwards. Many moralists would extend the time up to three hours.

    My father was dead less then one hour. We have always been taught the body does not die for three hours, and I remained with my father for that time.

    The American Priests of today hide behind Vatican 11 when denying the Faithful, and after 30 years there are few books that inform the Catholic People of the actual rules and rites. The Baltimore Catechism is no longer allowed in the today church. What is the book of reference for the Catholic who wants to know all the new so called laws? It seems the American Bishops interrupt the new Canon Laws according to their personal, social and political views and not that of the Roman Catholic Church. I would like to know which laws are optional, which are absolute and which are left to the discretion of the Bishop?

    Cardinal Ratzinger we are a family who has always built our lives around Jesus Christ and His Church. In 1962 when the church was destroyed by Vatican 11, we did not change our values. The Church and her official teachings still remained the center of our lives.

The feeling of terror, anger and total rejection of this Church during our times of absolute need is indescriable. All Catholics of Faith see the Church being destroyed from within, but we will not give in to "EVIL". We still believe in Jesus Christ, His Church and His Beloved Mother Mary.

My father gave his entire life to the church. President of the Holy Name--10 years. Fourth Degree Knight of Columbus from age 21 He died at age 81. He sang in the church choir for 35 years. The President of Parish Council, Lector, and Retreat Captain. He founded Retreat Organization and took men for weekend retreats in Southern Maryland from 1949 to 1962. In 1966 he was diagnoised with Leukemia From that time on his health deteriorated, but he continued to work for the church as much as possible. Every aspect of my father's life was influenced by the church, and yet when he needed the church, the church turned away, and denied him his very <u>Heritage and Birth Right</u> as a Roman Catholic.

Cardinal Ratzinger I beg and plead your assistance. If not for my family, then another Catholic family in the same situation. How long will the Faithful have to suffer before the Pope and Cardinals act to rescue and restore the church of Jesus Christ? Will it take the Chastisement and Purification to restore the church? You don't have to be a prophet to see the time is very near. As I have heard Father Vincent Miceli say, "The True Catholic Faithful living and dying today are Martyr's for the Faith".

Jesus Christ is the same as He was and will be forever. <u>What right does Humans have to change His Laws and Sacraments?</u>

I sincerely thank you for your indulgence in this matter.

May 27, 1992

Dear Mrs. DAvis:

I am in receipt of a copy of the letter that you sent to His Eminence, Josef Cardinal Ratzinger. I received a copy of your letter via our auxiliary bishop, MOst Rev. David E. Foley who asked that I reply via him, nOt to your rash judgments and hysterical hearsay, but to the actual events of the morning of the death of your father at BAyside of Poquoson Nursing Home.

I would answer first and foremost that your traditionalist (not Traditional) prjudices shine forth like the sores on that Italian woman, so afflicted with cancer that it manifested itself externally on her bosom - which when touched by ST. Dominic, turned into a pearl - t'would be great if the same could happen in your case. There is no other explication of how you "remembered" that morning.

You noted that I arrived quickly. Thank you. I came as so as I received the call from the nursing home, just as I was finishing the 6:30 a. m. Liturgy. Notice that I came, not your mythical Langley AF base chaplain. I did what any pre byter would have done.

You call me Father James Quiñlaa. My name is Thoams J. Quinlan.

You say taht I walked into the room wearing a beige suitand brown shoes. So what? Jesus is often painted in pink and blue nightgowns. So what? Waht does this have to do with the pastoral care of the sick and dying, or the celebration of the Annointing of the Sick, vulgarly called the last rit by youself.

I did not say "that's it". I said: "That's all I can do now". Check your husband's memory. He was there.

I did not say "I do not come here often". What I said was: "In order that the residents there might receive the Sacrament EACH AND EVERY WEEK, our parish has appointed episcopally approved Extraordinary Ministers of the EUcharist, who le Mass at the end of the Communion Rite, and bring the Euchar directly to the residents, thus manifesting their Unity with the Faithful, just finishing up celebrating our 9;00 a. m. Mass, exhibiting to these sick and elderly the Unity that Holy Communion signifies and effects". I go there often to visit. EVery quarter or so we ahve a Communal Annointing of the Sick at this nursing home.

Your rash judgement and overt ignorance ofmyself and my ministry comes through strongly. Your BAptist and Methodist

-2-

friends seem more like yourself, an uptight crowd of know-nothings, sunken in the morass of Biblical literalism. They did not write to the paper about my errors. They wrote their fundamentalistic views, only exceeded by your traditionalist mish-mash. about the Genesis Myth, Chs. I - XI, 28. If you and they really think God made the world in sis days. Go ahead. If you think you are inferior to your husband and all other men (including me), because you were taken out of one of our ribs while we were having an extended nap, go ahead. If you think your gender is the cause of evil, go right on believing this hogwash.

How do YOU know that I do not DESERVE (??) the title of priest? Check the places where the word priest is used in the New Testament and HOW it is used. And your supreme arrogance is shown when you state that I am only interested in social issues and recycling. IN fact this shows you to be a damn fool! I spend less than 5% of my time on these facets of Gospel life. I have to spend 95% of my time on Liturgy Education, Planning, Administration, etc. in this parish. And how would YOU know anyway? You do not know me. You speak of my "reputation". Thank you. Do YOU have a reputation? If you do, I wouldn't know of it, or be interested in it, but certainly wouldn't judge it. JSUT THE FACTS M'AM, JUST THE FACTS!

ALso you do not seem to understand that Jesus, whom you and I both claim to love and imitate, spent most of his time, denouncing, attacking, correcting, and challenging the social issues, especially the disparities, of His Jewish economy and culture.

You claim that I am a disgrace to the CAtholic community. PLease document or keep quiet.

And not only do you attack me, but you attack our beloved and prophetic bishop, Walter F. Sullivan, *jure divino*, the eleventh bishop of Richmond. I do not undertand your problem with him and again your rash judgement of him. Do you have problems with the Apostolic Pro-Nuncio to the United States of America. It seems as tho you ahve problems with anyone who isn't as out of it as yourself.

You state that you are entitled to membership at Langley AF Base chapel. Good - go there and STAY there. But if you are so devoted to your chaplain-pastor, why didn't you call him? If my reputation is so bad, why would you even think of calling upon me for service (heretical service???)

Another blatant misconception - your father died before 7:00 a. m. according to the nurse. IN fact he must have died while I was celebrating the DIvine Liturgy. When I arrived your father had been dead for some time. In our church today we do not annoint cadavers. The sacramental principle has always been: SACRAMENTA PROPTER HOMINES, i. e., for the "living" Your citing an antedeluvian text adds nothing to your

THOLIC COMMUNITY OF POQUOSON AND TABB   POST OFFICE BOX 2100   POQUOSON VIRGINIA 23662   804/868-7877
THOMAS J. QUINLAN/PASTOR

complaint and attack. If I had had a doubt as to whether your father had JUST died, or if I am called to the scene of a sudden death, I might be tempted to use themodality of conditional administration of the Sacraments, but in the case of your father, he was stone "daid". Therefore I followed the pastoral care principles of the Roman CAtholic Church and recited all the prayers for the dead according to the norm promulgated by our present Holy FAther, John Paul II. (Cf. PASTORAL CARE OF THE SICK, Prayers for the Dead, pp. 223-229.) Also note, on page 221, the "official" Church states "A priest is NOT to administer the sacraments of penance or annointing. INSTEAD, he should pray for teh dead person using these orsimilar prayers.) GEt it????????????????????

You say that "WE WERE TAUGHT THIS AND THAT". Who is this WE? It seems more like your interpretation of what you have extricated more than any real WE - outside of YOUR imagination that is. ANd who tuaght you that the soul remains in the body three hours? What is the evidence you can proffer that the "soul" does not leave the body immediately when the signs of life cease. Where does it go? Does it take a nap? Does it experiment with transmigration, or romantically flirt with reincarnation?

It is shamefully obvious that you do not know, nor have you the faintest tinge of understanding of what you are saying. You speak of your father's body and soul as tho they wre two ontological beings. EVen the first year philosophy student knows that the BODY and SOUL are CO-PRINCIPLES OF BEING, SO CALLED ENTIA RATIONIS. This sytem of trying to obtain insight into the complicated beings that are us was devised by ARistotle and "baptized" by SAint Thoas Aquinas. This system of metaphysics did help givwe us some peeps into, some tational supports so to speak, into our Divine Faith. These are not and could not be TEACHINGS of the Roman CAtholic Churc This system endured for about eight-hundred years and came to be called the PHILOSOPHIA PERENNIS, except it ain't PERENNIS no mo';And one should only use it and its terminology if one understands that it is based upon the epistemological principle of the Analogy of Proportionality, albeit intrinsic.. Fr. Kenneth Baker, S. J., whom you cite, is a nice priest and a quaint PAMPHLETEER, but he is no theologian. He's more the CAtholic Digest, BAltimore CAtechism, quickie essayistic journalist.

You say your father was CAtholic to the core. Wonderful! You say your father has "a heritage and a birth right" to be CAtholic. No one has that. He, like the rest of us, was s(e lected) by God to receive the GIFT of FAith. The more I reread your letter, the more hersies, not to mention nonsense, found, and quite cras at that.

You say that priests hid behind VAtican II. I am not hiding

-4-

behind anything except the Sacraments, the Bible, and the Church. You say that VAtican II ruined the Church. This is what I mean when I say that you appear to be a DAMN FOOL. How did you arrive at the judgement (more arrogant than any 20 heretics in history) that VAtican II is not an authentic ecumenical council of the One, Holy, CAtholic, and Apostolic Church??????

By what right do you opt for twenty and leave out the twenty first council? Has the prophet Maroni revealed this to you? You seem to know more than Cardinal Ratzinger and Pope John Paul II put together!

Your threats of chastisement and purification are daily doses on Pat Robertson's show, and people of that ilk. Why don't you join the 700 CLub? And your talk about "not having to be a prophet to see that the time is near" - come off it. That is nothing more than omni-recurring cheap Psuedo-Adventism.

When you find out the Third Fatima Secret, call me up.

May the Lord curse your arrogance, ignorance, and judgemental attitude! May the Lord bless you in your simpleness!
AND MAY YOUR "SOUL" CLEAVE TO YOUR "BODY" FOR THREE YEARS!!!

Sincerely,

T.R.

(Rev.) Thomas J. Quinlan

June 6, 2002

Most Reverend Walter F. Sullivan D.D.
811 Cathedral Place
Richmond, VA 23220-4801

Dear Bishop Sullivan,

My wife and I attended 11 AM mass at The Church of The Holy Family in Virginia Beach on June 2, 2002. The Pastor, Thomas J. Quinlan, presided and gave the sermon. We would like to tell you of his teachings on that day. It seems that he has some personal issues which unfortunately affect his teachings.

We believe that his teachings are heretical. We feel obligated to somehow apprise those, both Catholic and non-Catholic, that could be scandalized by his false teachings that he does not teach what the Catholic Church believes and teaches.

While you may have received earlier inputs regarding Fr. Quinlan's teachings we will briefly describe them as they were presented June 2, 2002. He preached that we do not have souls. He expressed contempt for the concept of transubstantiation and stated that Jesus becomes present in the Eucharist, not through power passed to him from a bishop, but through three steps, the final one being the approval of the congregation by their Amen. He likened it to the Church's teaching that the Sacrament of Marriage is administered by the people being married. He stated that he was not a priest, that there are no priests but Jesus. TQ'S NOTES in the bulletin of June 1/2, 2002 stated that Jesus did not found a hierarchical church.

While perhaps not heretical he expressed his contempt for the Roman Catholic Church during most of its' history, for Pope Pius X, and for adoration of the Blessed Sacrament. His entire sermon had a contemptuous tone to it. It was also crude and vulgar as evidenced by his use of the words hell, damn (neither used in a religious sense), crap, and by pointing out that Jesus is present in our bodies when we receive the Eucharist and thereafter in the latrine as a natural consequence of eating and drinking.

Thank you for reading this letter. Our prayers are for you and the Church you represent in Virginia, especially that your love of the Church and of your flock will guide you in your pastoral actions.

Sincerely,

John F. Oppie
104 Lariat Drive
Georgetown, TX 78628

CC Fr. Thomas J. Quinlan, Pastor of Church of the Holy Family
    The Apostolic Nuncio to the United States, His Excellency, The Most Reverend Gabriel Montalvo J.C.D.

June 21, 2002

Mr. John F. Oppie
104 Lariat Drive
Georgetown, Texas 78628

Dear Mr. Oppie:

I was sorry to learn of your reaction to my homily on Sunday, June 2, 2002. I do not know where you got the impression that I have even a tinge of contempt for the Roman Catholic Church which I have loved and worked for these many years. Authentic love includes Gospel criticism.

But more important than your emotional impressions – a visitor from Texas at that – is your complaint to our bishop and the Apostolic Pronuncio that I am a heretic. There can be no more serious charge.

I can intuit from your statements that you are a sort of Opus Dei, pre-Tridentine traditionalist, which is fine with me. You have a conventional grasp of the Faith which you learned as a child.

Now as to the alleged "heresies:"

1. We do not have souls. THAT IS CORRECT. Body and soul are <u>ENS RATIONIS</u>, I.E., CONCEPTS IN THE MIND only, invented by Aristotle to help explicate the complexity of the simultaneous fleshiness and spiritedness of every human begin. It was "baptized" by Saint Thomas Aquinas to help us understand our human nature and used in theology to gain some little insight into the Mysteries of our Faith. It was never to be taken literally because neither the body nor the soul have any real existence outside the mind – no matter the use of these terms in the Bible, theology, poetry, and love songs.

2. Transubstantiation is not a teaching of the Catholic Church. THAT IS CORRECT. It is one of several metaphysical concepts that pertain to the Aristotelian-Thomisitic system. There are many other insights (not explanations) of Jesus' Real Presence in the Eucharist. Other theologians prefer Transignification or Transfinalization. And all these only have significance for those who know how to use the epistemological tools of the analogy of proportionality, and that extrinsic!

The Church is honest. She uses the words "eucharistically present" to avoid confusion and keeps the Mystery a mystery.

3. I do not believe that the power passed on to me by a bishop, archbishop, cardinal, or Pope "confects" the Eucharist. THAT IS CORRECT. I was trying to explain the various facets of the Real Presence with its elements, sc.:
    1.) The Invocation of the Holy Spirit (Epiklesis)
    2.) The words (or similar) words of Institution recited by the presbyter, and

3.) The confirmation of the presence of the Body and Blood of the Resurrected Lord by the Body of Christ standing around the altar in the Great Amen.

You perhaps think that the priest's recitation of the words of Institution alone zap Jesus down onto the altar.

N.B. Our Church has just accepted as valid the Eastern-rite Liturgy that has an epiklesis and Great Amen and NO words of institution as a valid Mass!!!

4. That the ministers of the Sacrament of Marriage are the bride and groom. THAT IS CORRECT. You didn't think the minister of this sacrament was the priest did you? Even the antediluvian Irish Catechism taught that in the last century.

5. That I am not a priest – that there are no priests in the New Testament – that the Risen Christ is the only high priest of the new and everlasting covenant. THAT IS CORRECT. All ordained in our church are presbyters. Cf. The revised rite of ordination, I Peter, etc. And that even Jesus is the high priest is an analogy of faith; in Heaven as our sole Mediator. Every baptized Christian is a "priest." Priests, temples, and of course animal sacrifice have all been abrogated by Jesus.

6. That Jesus did not found an hierarchical church. THAT IS CORRECT. Hierarchical systems are all post-Constantinian. Jesus founded a movement, albeit Church, that is egalitarian (beyond Jeffersonian dreams) in nature, and beautifully differentiated by billions of charisms and gifts.

You could be charged with many heresies. But to have a Church trial for you we would have to show that you know something about our Church's teachings, and you just wouldn't qualify.

If I thought you were a heretic, I would recommend that the Catholic Bishops' Conference of Texas tie you to a cactus and burn you on the prairie. But have no fear. You're just too out of it!

May the Holy Spirit within you prompt you to overcome your ignorance and aid you in vanquishing your arrogance.

T. Q.

(Rev.) Thomas J. Quinlan

cc: Most Rev. Walter F. Sullivan, Bishop of Richmond
Most Rev. Gabriel Montalvo, Apostolic Pronuncio to the USA

LORRAINE M. POGGIS
Road Runner Resort
5500 St. Lucie Boulevard
Ft. Pierce, Florida 34946

January 12, 2003

Rev. Thomas J. Quinlan, Pastor
Church of the Holy Family
1279 North Great Neck Road
Virginia Beach, Virginia 23454

Dear Father Quinlan:

I attended Mass at your Church of the Holy Family on December 29th, 2002 at 11 a.m. on the Feast of the Holy Family with my three (3) grandsons, ages 9, 15 and 16 together with their parents.

I was looking forward to hearing a Sermon about the Feast of the Holy Family and how important the family structure is especially since we all are bombarded from all sides with distractions that can pull apart our family unit and corrupt our children. Mary, Joseph and Jesus were and are an example to all of us. Jesus set an example by obeying his parents even though He knew what His role was and what it would be. His parents were loving and guiding.

Instead of an uplifting Sermon addressed to the children and their parents on the Feast of the Holy Family I heard you "babble on about "genitalia" and how you thought "Perhaps Hitler might have had the right idea." It was disgraceful!

Had I not had my grandsons with me at Mass I would have walked out of your Church in disgust! In all my years of going to Mass on Sundays and on a daily basis I have never ever had the urge to leave my church because of the rantings and ravings of a man of God. How could you even think, let alone mention that "Perhaps Hiltler might have had the right idea." and speak such an unconscionable thought especially with children present.

Had you wished to present that sermon it would have been a good idea if you had written it down on paper so that you at least might have been able to reread it and possibly edit it. If after rereading your sermon you still wanted to present it and I saw it I would have suggested that you send a copy to your Bishop so that he could have edited it. I wish I would have had a tape recorder so that your Bishop could have heard you and he would realized your sermon was really only fit for the trash bin!

It is difficult enough for Catholics who love their Church and Christ to have much respect for our priests lately especially in light of all the sexual abuse of our children by "supposed" men of God who sit on their thrones and pontificate and cover up at the expense of our children. Priests should be reaching out to their people in love and understanding now more than ever before and not be sarcastic.

Perhaps there is an excuse for your sermon. Sometimes senility takes hold and it was just a "senior moment" that you were having.!

Respectfully,

Lorraine M. Poggis

May 4, 2003

DEar Mrs. Poggis:

Re: your letter of January 12:

You say youc ame expecting such and such. Of course you did, because of your misunderstanding of what a homily is. It is least of all to fulfill YOUR expectations, especially since you have manifested in your letter a supremem ignorance of this section of SCripture, commonly known as the Infancy Legends, PUrchase a copy of Fr. Raymond E. Brown's paperback AN ADULT CHRIST AT CHRISTMAS.

You say taht you would have walked out if you had not had your grandsons with you. How phoney! You have the charism of prophecy (witnessing to the TRuth) - use it. You should have walked out (in your ignorance) and witnessed for your grandsons. What a missed opportunity!

You have a faddish idea called family strucutres. Cute, but without sexual and marital values, you are wasting ykour time talking about family values, because they presume the other two, which is the exact point of my homily. EVery politician, every unthinking mother (like you) talks about family values in order to avoid talking about teh deeper pre-conditions thereunto, sc., sexual and marital values. You might be one of those who calls bastards love children.

Your ignorance of Scripture is untenable. Read the above book. IN fact I would be willing to mail you one upon request. WE don't know a personal thing about the family. Joseph is an unknown. Mary has little known about her - only the important facets of her life which are related to Jesus, not herself. Once one knows and is honest about the Infancy Narratives of Matthew and Luke, Chapters I and II, pietistic slop is avoided. And you would ahve and should ahve "expected" something better.

I too wihs you had a tape recorder. OUr bishop would have starightened you out. You suffer from conventional FAith, a grandmother of some age with the FAith of a sixth grader. Your poor grandsons.

The sex abuse scandal ahs nothing to do with me. Go discuss it with them - they would ahve given you one of your expected, expectant sermons as you call homilies.

You say I am a "man of God". WEll you are a "woman of God". Thru BAptism we all are. What are you talking about? YOur antedeluvian attitude towards clericalism!

Your nasty comment about senility applies much more to yourself than to myself. Homilies are for adults. Obviously you don't wualify.

Praying that you will mature before death!

TQ

(Rev.) Thomas J. Quinlan

FIRE ENGINE MARY

8761 Irish Road
Faber, Va. 22938
January 21, 2003

Bishop Sullivan
811 Cathedral Place
Richmond, Va. 23220

Bishop Sullivan:

On December 31, my wife and I were in Virginia Beach and decided to attend Mass on the eve of the Holy day. There are several Churches in the area, as you know, and we selected Holy Family. That turned out to be a terrible mistake.

The celebrant was a Rev? Thomas Quinlan, who should be removed immediately from his priestly responsibilities.

He started with an opening remark of no consequence, read the opening prayer and then did the Gloria (out of order, as you know). They were followed by two readings, selected by him (so he said in his "homily"), which were basically anti Semitic. In alluding to the two readings he proclaimed that the Old Testament was obsolete, as was Rosh Hashanah.

He then proceeded with the crux of his homily which consisted of lambasting the "schizophrenic hierarchy" of the Catholic Church for attempting to force the rules outlined in the new Roman Missal upon him and his congregation, that the Pope was just trying to "put us in our place", that no one is coming up to receive communion and sticking their tongue out at him, that he thanks the architect every day for creating a floor upon which it is almost impossible to kneel (pebbled cement), that no one is going to tell him or his parishioners what to do because "we know what we want".

I am almost 67 years old and my wife is 61. We looked at each other, sensing that we were not really in the presence of a sane man and for the first time in our lives, walked out of Mass. My only remark was to a lady usherette to whom I simply said, this man should be defrocked. Little did I know then how right I was.

We went to dinner at a family restaurant nearby and did not enjoy our meal very much because of what we had just experienced.

I decided, after dinner, to ask our waitress if she was familiar with Holy Family Church and their irreverent pastor. She said she was a member of that parish. We told her what had happened and she said many, many people have expressed their distaste of this man and disbelief in what he preaches. She then told us the following:

> It is a family habit (and a nice one) of saying a prayer whenever she or they hear a fire truck or ambulance siren. It happened that while driving with her sister and 7 year old niece, a rescue squad truck passed them and she turned to her niece and said let's say a Hail Mary. Her niece responded – oh we don't do that, Father Quinlan says "not to pray to Mary because She has no power".

We were dumbfounded. I asked if anyone had ever written to him about his anti Catholic, anti Pope, anti Blessed Mother opinions and preaching and she said many have. He prints the letters in the bulletin and writes scathing responses also in the bulletin.

The question now is what are you, Bishop Sullivan, going to do about this man? Are you going to overlook his negative preaching about the Blessed Mother? Are you going to tell us he does other things well? Are you going to continue to protect him as one of your "Golden Boys"? (That connotation is from a priest in the Diocese of Richmond), or are you going to act like a real Bishop and remove this sorry excuse for a priest from his pastorship and assign him to some cloister type facility where he can no longer do harm to parishioners, particularly impressionable children.

We discussed this with our sons who live out of state. One, residing in RI discussed it with his pastor who was shocked that Quinlan (I'm sorry, I cannot in good conscience call him Father) was still a Pastor, but wasn't surprised given the reputation of the Diocese of Richmond and its Bishop. What a sad statement!

Another son, in DC, has the ear of someone close to the U. S. Conference of Catholic Bishops and he has informed them of this situation, as we will via a copy of this letter.

I also spoke to two other priests of this Diocese who told me about him going on the altar dressed as Superman, about riding a fork lift or volkswagon, depending on who you talk to, down the aisle and that you were made aware of these actions and did little or nothing about it. Your office also told me there have been many complaints about this man.

Don't you think that it is time to take action?

Please do not even insult us with any other response other that you have removed this man from his or any other pastorship or parish.

We will remain faithful to our Church and our Lord regardless, however.

Mary and Jon ten Hoopen

cc: Archbishop Gabriel Montalvo, Washington, DC
Rev. Msgr. John J. Strynkowski, Washington, DC
Derek ten Hoopen, Pittsford, New York
Raymond ten Hoopen, W. Bay Shore, New York
Douglas ten Hoopen, Newport, RI
Jonathan ten Hoopen, Washington, DC
Charles & Mary Kate Adams, Stuart, Fla.

May 12, 2003

Mary and Jon ten Hoopen
8761 Irish Road
Faber, Virginia 22938

Dear Mary and John:

I am in receipt of your letter to Bishop Sullivan, our ordinary. I thank you for your interest. So many Catholics are indifferent.

In these United States of America our bishops long ago replaced the European tradition of Epiphany with the valiant attempt to try to set aside the first day of each new year as a holy day. Pastoral considerations and the culture of the day influenced them to request this change from the universal Church's celebration of Epiphany.

I did not say the hierarchy was schizophrenic but that this feast day with its constantly changing names and superimposition of irrelevant readings and prayers undermined the original purpose that the bishops intended: sc., that New Year's Day be dedicated to God as a sort of Catholic Rosh Hashanah. When I was in Rome for a sabbatical my intuition of pastoring was substantiated by a Vatican liturgiologist who taught the class – the so-called feast of the Solemnity of Mary has the worst readings of the church year. Is it New Year's Day or is it Mary's Day, or in yesteryear, was it Jesus' all-important Circumcision? It is a problem for pastors, liturgists, and most importantly the People of God who come on that day.

I never said, nor even thought, that the Old Testament, better Hebrew Scriptures, were obsolete. Like all Roman-rite liturgies we had an Old Testament reading.

We object as do most honest Catholics to the new "rubrics" because they are an attempt to reclericalize Mass. Is the presbyter holier than the people????? And if he isn't, so what? We do not want to fall into a recurring heresy: that the efficacy of a Sacrament depends upon the morality or worthiness of the priest or Pope, in which latter case we wouldn't have any Sacraments left!

Your fairy tale about the waitress is most creative. It reminds one of the hagiography of the Dark Ages, e.g., when saints were supposed to have refused sucking their mothers' breasts on the Wednesdays and Fridays of Lent. Your waitress, let's call her Fire-Engine Mary, manifested her immature faith. But the seven year old niece should be declared a Doctor of the Church, since she understands prayer unlike her aunt, the waitress. When she prophesied: "Oh, we don't do that (say a Hail Mary at siren screaming time), Father Quinlan says not to pray to Mary because she has no power." What a grace-filled intelligent child! No Catholic prays to the Blessed Mother. And Mary has no "power" separated from Jesus.

I have never been a Golden Boy of any bishop, believe me.

There is nothing wrong with our bishop or the diocese of Richmond.

I also remain faithful to our Church and to the Lord.

TQ

(Rev.) Thomas J. Quinlan

March 24, 2003

Reverend Thomas J. Quinlan
Church of the Holy Family
1279 North Great Neck Road
Virginia Beach, VA 23454

Dear Father Quinlan:

I was stunned to see the solicitation for prayers for Stephen Baggerly in the March 22/23 church bulletin, but have followed the suggestion to pray for the coward.

I pray that he has an extended period of isolation to reflect upon his unlawful acts that could have potentially increased the risks to the patriotic men and women courageous enough to risk the ultimate sacrifice to permit spineless idiots like him to shame the country that gives him the freedoms he perverts.

Sincerely,

James R. Healy

cc: S. Baggerly

March 28, 2003

Dear Mr. Healy:

Thank you for your letter of concern about requesting prayers for Steve Baggerly.

As you ought to know, there are two EQUAL moral positions about War in the Catholic Church, going all the way back to St. Martin of Tours, who came from a military family, was abducted by his pagan father back to the base where he should have been serving for the Emperor, because he refused to fight based upon the Gospel of Peace. In every century we have had numerous pacifists, including St. Francis of Assisi, and Dorothy Day (who was also called a Communist). All this was reflected upon last Monday night at Adult Education class. At each and every Mass we pray for our soldiers, sailors, and marines. Seeking prayers for a pacifist who is also a conscientious objector is in total consonance with Catholic morality, based upon the Gospel. Just as there are many conditions to even consider a modern war JUST, so one of the conditions for conscientious objectors is that if they break the civil law, they must pay the legal penalty. He is.

Steve is not a "spineless idiot" as you recklessly name-call him. To protest a war that is unjust in one's conscience is just as patriotic as anyone risking her/his life in Iraq. You seem to need as much education and reflection time as Steve.

Sincerely,

T. Q.

(Rev.) Thomas J. Quinlan
Pastor

Dr. David Allen White, Ph.D.
Professor of Literature, Annapolis Naval Academy

J.M.J.

Saturday, July 5, 2003
Our Lady's First Saturday

Dear Father Quinlan,

As a convert to the Catholic faith, I have witnessed with profound grief the sufferings of the Church to which, by God's grace, I was drawn late in life. Like many Catholics who are aggrieved by the current ecclesial crisis, which seems to deepen with each new revelation of scandal, I ask myself the question, "What is the *cause* of it all?" Thoughtful Catholics today are seeking an answer to this question that is rather more precise than "Original Sin."

Yes, of course, the sin of Adam is at the root of every problem of the human condition, including the crisis that now convulses the human element of the Church. But where this crisis is concerned, a much more immediate and specific cause seems to be at work. Many Catholics are coming to the realization that *something* happened about forty years ago that set the crisis in motion -- an event, or a complex of events, that has led to unprecedented upheaval, confusion and even loss of faith among the members of the Church today.

Indeed, the sudden and precipitous decline in the Church's vital statistics in every category -- vocations, conversions, marriages, baptism, Mass attendance -- beginning around 1960, has led a growing number of Catholics to conclude, if only intuitively, that the crisis in the Church has a particular cause emanating from that time.

And now a widely acclaimed new book, *The Devil's Final Battle*, has provided the confirmation of this widespread intuition. This compelling work demonstrates with overwhelming documentation that the current crisis was predicted in its particulars not only by one of the great popes of modern times, Pius XII (whose prophetic remarks as recounted in the book will stun you), but by the Mother of God Herself in a series of apparitions the currently reigning Pope has endorsed with the full weight of his office.

It was, in fact, John Paul II who told us in his sermon at Fatima, Portugal in 1982 that the Message of Fatima "imposes an obligation" on the Church. It was John Paul II who, on that occasion, linked the Fatima prophecies to "the immensity of human suffering...to the almost apocalyptic menaces looming over the nations and mankind as a whole." John Paul even found in the Fatima prophecies (as he said in his sermon at Fatima in May 2000) the fulfillment of Chapter 12 of the Book of the Apocalypse, with its fearsome warning about the "tail of the dragon" dragging consecrated souls to their ruin.

The Devil's Final Battle demonstrates beyond any doubt that one cannot make sense of the current crisis in the Church and the world, or find its ultimate solution, without a clear understanding of what the Mother of God confided to Her Church at Fatima.

God's interventions in human history are not in vain. The papal endorsements of Fatima mean that every Catholic must recognize that God has spoken to the Church of our time at Fatima, and that in order to bring an end to the ecclesial and world crisis, we must heed the message He has conveyed to us through His Mother. The book you will soon receive is a great stride in that direction.

I am so persuaded of the importance of *The Devil's Final Battle* that I am arranging to have it sent to you free of charge, with the urgent plea that you read it, ponder it, and pass it along to others.

I am enclosing a brochure with many other endorsements of the book written by priests and laity. This brochure is put out by the Militia of Our Immaculate Mother, who are promoting this book. You can obtain extra copies from them, if you would like.

These reviewers are unanimous in their conclusion that *The Devil's Final Battle* is an extraordinary exposition of the truth of our situation. Only when we face up to that truth can we begin in earnest the process of restoring the Church and bring peace, true peace, to a warring world. For the truth is that the Mother of God has given us the way out of the crisis, if only we will take it.

Soon you will be receiving your personal copy of *The Devil's Final Battle*. I implore you with all my heart to take the time to read the book and to act on what it says -- for the good of the Church and of all humanity.

Respectfully yours in Christ,

Dr. David Allen White

P.S. Your free book should arrive within the next couple of weeks. Please don't miss this great opportunity -- read it as soon as you can.

July 22, 2003

Dear Mr. White:

I am in receipt of your letter and pamphlet of July 5.

I was very disappointed in it because even though you are in no wise a professor of biblical literature, you are a professor of literature, and that should have connaturally steered you away from a fundamentalism which is all through your letter.

You state that of course the sin of Adam is the cause of every problem of the human condition. You also state gratuitously that thoughtful Catholics today are seeking an answer that is rather more precise than "Original Sin."

You say simultaneously that original sin is the cause of evil, but now you are going to make it more precise. I doubt it. Properly demythologized (and as a professor of literature you should understand the term full well) there is no such <u>tertium quid</u> as the "Fall," a devil, etc. You are just handing on more medieval Aristotelian-Thomistic, and indeed Augustinian ideas which no longer wash. No only do they not mesh with contemporary knowledge (not theories), but all the way back in the twelfth century we had another entire school of thought about Jesus, why he came (the final motivation of the Incarnation by John Duns Scotus, to mention one) which has nothing to do with your so-called "original sin."

Not only are you confused about evil, original sin, devil, but you wade into private revelations of Mary which are outside the scope of Catholic Faith, no matter John Paul II's devotion to Fatima, not to mention his egregious error of messing up the Easter Cycle in the liturgical year with his Divine Mercy Sunday, influenced by that Polish wild woman, Sr. Faustina. If you believe in Our Lady of Fatima, fine. I and millions of other Catholics do not. We believe that the Blessed Mother was "assumed" (whatever that means in a post-metaphysical corpus of thought) into Heaven. There she remains. All remain there with the exception of Jesus who will come back at the Parousia.

Your misinterpretation of the Book of Revelation is unforgivable because of your secular knowledge and position. You sound like Pat Robertson. You should take a literary course apocalyptic literature to help you understand Revelation, II Isaiah, Judith, Daniel, and parts of Ezekiel and Zechariah.

Your "Final Battle" sounds like silly Mormon talk. Every day is the final battle for whomever happens to be alive. Your fundamentalistic approach smacks of Pope Sylvester III who in the year 1000 C.E. inflicted abstinence on the whole Church because he thought that the end of the world was coming then. Now is 2000 and we have a new bunch of ignoramuses predicting the final day and the final battle of the devil, and other Sodom and Gomorrah syndromes.

I really do feel sorry for you because you seem to have come under some anti-intellectual influence, which is antithetical to your position, your knowledge, your Catholic (??) Faith.

Sincerely,

Thomas J. Quinlan

(Rev.) Thomas J. Quinlan
Pastor

Warren E. Boisselle
734 Sir Walter Circle
Virginia Beach, Virginia 23452
Tel: 757-340-5874

June 27, 2003

Barbara Hughes MFS
945 Amesbury Rd
Virginia Beach, VA 23464

Dear Ms. Hughes,

"**Three faiths encouraged in dialogue to learn from each other.**" This is the title of the article that appeared in the Catholic Virginian.

I am curious, Ms. Hughes, just what did you learn from Islam? Did you learn that there are errors in the Bible? Does Islam help you find flaws in the words of Jesus? If Jesus is wrong about some of His words, then as God, He surely knew He was wrong, therefore, He intended to deceive. Jesus would have to be lying. Are you suggesting that Jesus is a liar?

Rabbi Panitz said, "*We have much in common with respect to content of faith. We believe there's one God, that God is the creator of all the universe, that God is the redeemer.*" How can God, a spirit, be a redeemer for the sins of man? Can God be both the offended one and the redeemer at the same time? Why has the Church lied to us all these years by telling us that it is **Jesus** who died to redeem our sins? Does not consorting with the enemy also make the Church a liar and deceiver?

During every mass, the creed is part of the liturgy. Based on your ideas, this creed is very hypocritical. Pay attention the next time you recite. All of the mass is based on a person of God that neither of your cohorts in dialogue believe in. In my opinion, you have abrogated your privilege to call yourselves "Christian," followers of Christ.

Your dialogue makes a mockery of Christ who said that none can go to the Father but through Him. You make a mockery of the apostles who followed the command of Christ to go forth and preach His word throughout the world. You make fools out of all Christians and martyrs who died for their faith in Christ. You make buffoons out of all missionaries who obeyed the directive of Christ: "*Go ye therefore, and teach all nations, baptizing them in the name of the Father, and of the Son, and of the Holy Ghost; teaching them to observe all things whatsoever I have commanded you: and, lo, I am with you always, even unto the end of the world.*"

Your dialogue makes you hypocrites and charlatans. You would compromise your soul for a delusion of peace on earth. If peace on earth were to be possible, Jesus would not have to come again. Read again Luke 12:51-53. "*Suppose ye that I have come to give peace on earth? I tell you nay. . . .*" You will not allow the facts to get in the way of your ideologies and fantasies. Pity! You are the Pied Piper and the false prophet leading the sheep to their destruction.

Sincerely,

July 19, 2003

Dear Mr. Boisselle:

I do not know where you are coming from. You are all over the lot and misquoting Church documents, the Bible, etc.

To answer your specific rantings:

1. Islam doesn't help me or Mrs. Hughes. We are not Muslims, but wonderful Catholics. WE are interested in Islam because it, together with the Catholic Church, each have 1,000,000 members and thus are poised to influence the 21st century. Muslims, like us, believe in
One God whom they call Allah. The Jews call him Jahweh, and we call Him/Her God-in-Jesus. That's a similarity we can all work on together. Good.

2. Rabbi Panitz was using redeemer in a different sense than we do. They have a completely different idea about redemption. Also, remember that Jesus came to die for our sins and redeem us is ONE theology. There are others, like the Franciscan theology of Duns Scotus that teaches that Jesus did not come to die on account of our sins, but only to complete creation, i. E., He would have come anyway. You are being too apodictical about things you do not seem to know much about'

3. The Creed has nothing to do with this dialog. Creeds come and go according to the present heresies. We need a new creed to summarize the heresies of traditionalists like yourself. There is nothing in our creeds against Islam,

4. 'To make disciples of all nations" is a commandment of Jesus. But we have to do it respecting human freedom, not by telemarketing or force. The Gospel is invitatory, i. E., IF you WISH   to be my disciple.

Jesus respected human freedom totally.

Muslims, Jews and Christians should all live together peacefully on this planet. Since each one thinks that they have the absolute truth, then let them dialog. Some will be converted to the other group. Fine. We believe that Jesus is the Jewish Messiah. We believe that He is the end-all and be-all of all of life, that He is the center of history. We try to convince others of this, but at the same time appreciate where they are coming from, respecting what they believe, and wishing that they will see what we see and join us. That's our hope, not our thrust.

I hope you can do some homework.

Sincerely,

T.Q.
(Rev.) Thomas J. Quinlan

27 July, 2003

Dear Father Quinlan,

Thank you for your prompt and heart felt response to my letter regarding the meeting held at your church entitled "Women Called, Women Silenced" advertised in the Virginian Pilot. I greatly respect your point of view and I can assure you I do not make it a habit to challenge priests on points of theology. Honestly, that was the first time I had ever written a priest for that reason. I greatly respect priests and love the sacrament of Ordination. I have four wonderful sons and pray that one or more of them may be called to the priesthood. It is for that reason that I feel compelled to respond to your action to support this meeting. I hope you will now allow me to respond to your letter.

Let me start by asking if you have ever read Pope John Paul II's letter *Ordinatio Sacerdotalis* dated May 22, 1994? As a priest I would think you would be greatly interested in what our Pontiff teaches about the subject of Priestly Ordination. I have included a copy of this letter. It is short and a very good read. Father, the Pope contradicts many of the reasons you stated about why we should be open to the possibility of women priests. You stated in your letter: "I hope you will be a little more careful in your use of the word Magisterium". What was your point? That the priestly ordination of men alone is not a teaching of the Magisterium? The Holy Father states clearly in this letter that it is in the Magisterium! Here are his words:

"Although the teaching that priestly ordination is to be reserved to men alone has been preserved by the constant and universal Tradition of the Church and *firmly taught by the Magisterium* (italics added) in its more recent documents, at the present time in some places it is nonetheless considered still open to debate, or the Church's judgment that women are not to be admitted to ordination is considered to have a merely disciplinary force. Wherefore, in order that all doubt may be removed regarding a matter of great importance, a matter which pertains to the Church's divine constitution itself, in virtue of my ministry of confirming the brethren (cf. Lk 22:32) I declare that the Church has no authority whatsoever to confer priestly ordination on women and *this judgment is to be definitively held by all the Church's faithful.* (italics added)"

My goodness Father! How more clear can the Holy Father be in this matter. Do you consider yourself to be among the Church's faithful? I am incredulous that you could so cavalierly state in your letter: " Mrs. Johnson did not meet with any overt intention of challenging the teaching of the

Church, if you can call it a teaching. It's really a practice." Father, those are your words and they are in direct opposition to our Holy Father and the constant teaching of the Church. Are you totally ignorant of this important letter regarding your priestly office, or are you totally in opposition to the teaching of our Pope? Which is it? I don't see any other alternative. You also stated "Yesterday's error is often tomorrow's teaching". Wow. Let me ask you bluntly Father, do you even recognize the teaching authority of the Church? Do you believe in the hypostatic union, the true presence of Christ in the Eucharist, the bodily resurrection of Jesus, the immaculate conception of Mary and other Magisterial teachings? Or do you believe that these teachings are merely "cultural applications" of their times that are open for debate among the faithful, or will be proven to be in error once we all are enlightened by persons such as Mrs. Johnson? Your examples of Freemasons, cremation, and other past disciplines of the Church miss the mark because they have never been Magisterial teachings. Magisterial teachings can not contradict each other. The Holy Father, in union with his Bishops, is protected by the Holy Spirit when teaching from the Chair of Peter in matters of faith and morals. (I feel like I'm teaching 8th grade catechism here.)

Father, as you can tell, I am quite upset. I am a hairs breadth away from mailing a copy of your letter to our Bishop and to the Congregation for the Doctrine of the Faith. I will however, take a deep breath, and pray I am misunderstanding your position in this matter. Please reconsider your statements on this important issue. You owe it to yourself and your parishioners. Along with the print of the Holy Father's letter, I am enclosing a copy of a letter which explains the theological reasons for a male priesthood. The reasons are awesome and compelling. I downloaded the letter off of an excellent Catholic website: catholicexchange.com. Father, you and your parishioners are in my prayers. God bless you in your ministry.

Vincent Drouillard
1032 Sandoval Dr.
Virginia Beach, VA
23454

July 17, 2003

Dear Mr. Drouillard:

I thank you for your concern in your letter of July 7, 2003.

First of all, I was unaware of the ad in the Virginian Pilot as I was away on vacation.

Secondly, I am well aware of the statement of Pope John Paul II that women can never be ordained.

Thirdly, I am familiar with the statement in the CCC.

The session by Mrs. Johnson last Sunday had to do with Women's Ministry in the Church. There is nothing wrong with that. She did state that she believed women should be ordained. That's her opinion and she is entitled to it. Others agreed with her. People have a right to discuss anything they want. She knows the official teaching, but disagrees with it. A knowledge of church history shows that yesterday's error is often tomorrow's teaching. Besides, the question of the ordination of women is not one of Faith, or Dogma, but of cultural application of the first-century Hellenistic Jewish texts of the New Testament. We are not fundamentalists or Mormons. Our teachings do not drop out of the sky. They are carefully discerned, interpreted, and RE-INTERPRETED by our Church.

Celibacy for a thousand years in the Western Church. No celibacy in the Eastern churches REQUIRED FOR ORDINATION. (Ruthenism-rite priests who choose to marry are no longer suspended by Rome.)

Deaconesses for several centuries. No deaconesses for many centuries. May be restored in this century.

No cremation for centuries. Approved and with a special rite today.

No membership in the Freemasons for four hundred years. O.K. today.

What's your point?

Mrs. Johnson did not meet with any overt intention of challenging the teaching of the Church, if you can call it a teaching. It's really a practice.

Discussion, dialog, reflection, discernment, prayer are all good for the "soul."

Also, I hope you will be a little more careful in your use of the word Magisterium. There are many sources of our Faith (we are not Bible-alone Protestants), but each source requires some distillation to be truly comprehended. I enclose a little schema for your reading.

Sincerely,

(Rev.) Thomas J. Quinlan
Pastor

Dear Rev. Thomas J. Quinlan:

We are a couple with three small kids coming from Spain 3 months ago.

At the very beginning I was delighted for having found a catholic parish so close to our house. We became members of the Holy Family with a big enthusiasm and looking forward to commit ourselves with our catholic parish.

But little by little, we became really disappointed due to your special way to see all those things coming from the Bishop of Rome.

This man, in his eighties, went to Spain in June and gathered 1.000.000 youngest coming from all spots of my country and the next day the same amount went to celebrate the Sunday mass.

We realized that you are really far from this Bishop that, you like him or not, leads the Catholic Church and in my view you should invent your own Church but not misunderstand those like me brand new in Great Neck.

In my humble view, when a catholic person goes to mass, he is looking forward to listening the Gospel of God and get this Word properly explained to be perfect as He was perfect. This person does not like to hear your fights against the Rome's way. I think that you should transmit your opinion to those in hierarchy in charge of it.

Trust me Rev. Thomas J Quinlan I am not interested in how the Church nominates Bishops (election or voting), I am interested in becoming perfect as Him.

I am not interested in share with you your idea about the distinction between clerics and the rest of people.

By the way, such distinction is not longer correct since Saint Jose Maria Escriva de Balaguer saw The Opus Dei and all the Catholics, with different vocations, have the same aim: Become Saint. Different vocation same target, this is the key and not your distinction that it could be everything but clear.

Please lead your people through the Catholic Roman path or create your own church, you'll be one more among so many in this country, because the Word of the Lord and our Tradition is assumed only by the Bishop of Rome.

By the present letter we leave your Church and we are really delighted for having found others that trust John Paul II and see him as the leader of the Catholic Church according to Our Lord Word and the Tradition. Your view will be very exciting but in other Church.

I request from you to forward this letter to the Bishop of Richmond or providing me his address to.

Yours sincerely,

Antonio Fragua

November 14, 2003

Dear Mr. Fraga:

You are absolutely correct when you say that any Catholic person goes to Liturgy to listen to the Gospel. You are most incorrect when you say that the homilist must agree with the bishop of Rome. That has never happened in history . When the bishop of Rome teaches anti-Gospel, antedeluvian, or irrelevant teachings, he stands to be criticized by the members of the church. Our disagreeing with him or our outright critiquing of him in no way lessens our loyalty and devotion to him as Vicar of Peter (not Vicar of Christ), his important Chair of Authority, etc. You are confusing the the office and the person.

Your citing of Escrive is interesting. He founded the KGB of the Catholic Church (OPUS DEI) which has temporary influence and power over the bishop of Rome. This group started off wonderfully and I knew many fabulous members of this "Order" in the 60s, but like so many other societies they became drunk with power and influence. They are fundamentalist spies, trying, out of misguided spirituality, to take our church back to a Pre-Trdentine era, if not further.

I am tryiing to lead my people to what is the real Church of both early Christianity and contemporary understanding of this universe. You are pre Christopher Columbus. I'm happy you didn't fall off the planet when you got to Gibraltar!

Like many Old World and Old Church people you are most arrogant, judgemental, and locked in your Indo-European caves.

You have no sense of your own corrupt identity and corroded roots:

You who are a descendant of the Inquisition

You who are from a country that persecuted the Jews and forced them (against the invitatory words of Jesus) to convert (thank God those Castilians, Ferdinand and Isasbella are out of the sainthood track).

You who raped South America, physically, sexually, economically, and ecclesiastically

You who built the Escorial under the patronage and to the "Honor" (???) of Generalissimo Franco, that brutal dictator and cohort of Mussolini and Hitler

You who are a descendant of the conquistadores who stole gold from every Indian they ever encountered to place it your glistening shrine-churches, reminiscent of temple worhsip abrogated by Jesus. (Cf. Toldeo and Castile).

You who belong to a people , who, if they ever took Church seriously and pretended to lead Catholic lives, would require the building of 400 more churches in Madrid alone

You who are a madding crowd of bull-killers, bull-runners, and bull-shitters!!!

May St. Peter Claver, a real Spanish saint, draw you back to the Gospel and the authentic Catholic Church, not the decadent Hispanic Church ya'll have come to be.

Weeping over the Iberian peninsula, I am

(Rev.) Thomas J. Quinlan

C: Most Rev. Walter F. Sullivan

His Eminence William Cardinal Keeler
Archbishop of Baltimore
320 Cathedral Street
Baltimore, MD 21201

Dear Cardinal Keeler,

My name is Mary Cabral, I live in San Jose, California, but I am originally from Virginia, the Tidewater area to be exact. I have two daughters that live in Virginia Beach, and I visit them quite often.

I usually go to Mass in Portsmouth where I grew up, since my daughters no longer attend the Catholic Church, I go by myself. Last Easter I attended a "Catholic" church (I thought) near my oldest daughter's new home she had just moved into. I went to Holy Family Church in Virginia Beach, and had to ask the person next to me if indeed I was in a Catholic Church? What I saw was horrendous and shocking, people acting out scences from the Wizard of Oz, it seemed so trivialized in light of our Lord's passion and death.

I could not believe the amount of money that had gone into that production, there were hundreds of yellow bricks that you had to walk down to get to your seat, and the costumes were something out of a major hollywood production. In the middle of Mass "Dorothty " came out and sang "Somewhere Over the Rainbow", dog included under her arm. The alter was adorned with green sparkling lights. There was no mention of Jesus Christ, only of the great and powerful Oz.

I did not say anything to my daughter at the time because she already had enough reason not to attend a Catholic Church, I didn't want to give her any more ammunition. I did share my information with my priest here in California, and he was shocked and said that I would never see anything like that here.

This Christmas, my youngest daugthter had called and said she was planning to attend Midnight Mass. She lives close to Star of the Sea, which I have been to, and enjoy very much. I just assumed that she was going there. The next morning I got a phone call from her, and she was quite confused. She ended up going to Holy Family Church, because Star of the Sea did not have a Midnight Mass, but in her mind, a Catholic Church is a Catholic Church anywhere. WRONG!

My daughter told me that the priest was saying awful things, using curse words, that Jesus was not born in Bethlehem, and no one should go to Bethlehem because it was dirty, and like a three ring circus. Someone got up to leave and a screaming match started between the priest and the person leaving. I then told her of my experience with this church at Easter, and that is not what our Church is all about.

I then went on line to check out more on this parish, and what I found out was even more shocking, I could go into details, from people calling this priest (TQ) as he wants to be called, wierd, ignorant and arrogant.
I would like for you to check out this web site and read "TQ"'s notes, and how his teaching is NOT in line with the Catechism of the Catholic Church, he is a brazen heretic.

The web site is http://www.holyfamilyvb.org------click on Questions & Discussions, then go to Discussion Forum. the rest will speak for itself.

You might wonder why I am so concerned with the Diocese of Richmond. There are many reasons, first I am sick to see my religion defiled and God's house used as an amusement center, the second reason is that I will be moving back to the Virginia Beach area in a year and a half. If we ever have to wonder why Catholics have stopped attending the Most Holy Sacrifice of the Mass.....this type of liturgical stupidity is clearly the answer.

I beg of you, Your Eminence to put a stop to this priest going uncensored, and help restore our traditional Catholic beliefs back into the Church.

Sincerely,

Mary Cabral
5841 Tandera Ave.
San Jose, CA 95123
(408) 224-5109

cc. The Catholic Diocese of Richmond

Catholic Diocese of Richmond
Office of the Episcopal Vicar

Eastern Vicariate

His Eminence William Cardinal Keeler
Administrator of the Diocese of Richmond
320 Cathedral Street
Baltimore, MD 21201

Dear Cardinal Keeler:

I received your letter two weeks ago requesting that I respond to the concerns of Mrs. Mary Cabral of San Jose California after she visited Holy Family Parish in Va. Beach. I have delayed meeting with Fr. Tom Quinlan, the pastor of Holy Family, since he has recently been hospitalized after a cardiac episode. I did not think it wise to add to his stress at this time. As soon as he is back to full health, I will meet and discuss with him the contents of
her letter.

For the present, permit me to make a few general observations, which may be helpful in responding to Mrs. Cabral:
1, Fr. Quinlan is a very successful pastor in one of Va. Beach's largest parishes. He has been at Holy Family for nearly three years. During that time the number of registered parishioners has increased significantly in spite of his demands for registration there:

    a. All registered parishioners are expected to tithe a portion of their income each year, moving toward 10% after taxes and other charities. The weekly collection has doubled since he arrived. He is said to have the highest per capita income in the diocese of Richmond.

    b. All parishioners are expected to participate in a neighborhood house church where parish issues and concerns are expressed and then presented at the regular Council meeting.

    c. Parishioners are encouraged to devote a portion of their time to spiritual growth beyond Sunday Mass attendance; e.g., scripture and theological reading, attendance at adult formation classes after Mass or at Monday evening sessions. (hundreds do so every week) All parishioners are given a major book each year, a catechism, the lives of the saints, a new theological or scriptural book.)

    d. He insist on a major commitment from the parish to those in need; and therefore,
the parish has an outstanding outreach, giving a tenth of its income. This has resulted in several marvelous efforts. The most exciting being the building of

a school and paying of the annual salary of all teachers in their twin parish in Haiti, but there are many more local projects.

e. Every parishioner is expected to make a commitment to some ministry and most do. This gives an excitement to this parish with all participating in its efforts. They are proud of their parish. Its pastoral care of the sick and homebound is an inspiration to everyone in the city. Not only is there a full time minister to the sick, but also many parishioners and the pastor himself visit the large hospital in the parish and the fifteen nursing facilities. There is an average of three funerals a week.

f. Fr. Quinlan is the only priest in this parish. He has frequent calls to the local hospital, day and night, to minister to the sick and dying. Because of his care many families choose to have the funeral of a loved one at that parish since they are not registered elsewhere. This is his great work of evangelization.

g. Fr. Quinlan, in spite of being terribly overworked, has taken it upon himself to gather the younger pastors of Va. Beach for lunch once a month. This is the important ministry of mentoring young priests who are feeling very isolated these days.

There is much more, but that is a context in which to judge Mrs. Cabral's criticism. He is not run-of-the-mill, but those who know him well, know how much he loves the Church and calls it to purify itself.

<u>Now to Mrs. Cabral's criticism of the Liturgy at Holy Family:</u>

1. <u>The Wizard of Oz:</u> She thinks that the use of the Wizard of Oz last Lent and Holy Week was a trivialization of the Christian Mysteries we celebrate during that holy season. Actually, much like the teaching methodology of Jesus, it is the use of modern parable in order to help our generation understand the great themes of the Lenten readings. I celebrated one of the Sundays of Lent in 2003 and after the first reading there was a five or six line script to advance the theme that was begun on Ash Wednesday. I did not get the feeling that it was at a three-ring circus. On the contrary the people were very attentive and I can say that it helped me structure my homily on the scriptures that Sunday. I have provided a copy of the material on The Wizard of Oz, which was provided to every parishioner. The costumes were donated by a local theater at no charge to the parish. And, yes, professional actors did enact the story week by week, but those actors were also parishioners of Holy Family Parish

2. <u>The Christmas Midnight Mass:</u> I did hear about the incident that bothered the non-churchgoing daughter of Mrs. Cabral, but I was not there. I was told by some parishioners that Fr. Quinlan became upset when a visitor stood up during his homily and, while walking down the aisle shouted back to the ambo: "Shame on you!" When I asked Fr. Quinlan about this incident he said the man was upset by his challenge that the Infancy Narratives were not historical but theological statements. He said that apparently this man was shocked by that truth which he apparently never heard before. And yes, he admitted to making some comments in his homily about the terrible condition of the holy places at Bethlehem. But he

objected to her saying that he used curse words on Christmas. It was a brief incident in which the man screamed at him and he screamed back: "And Shame on you." That was all. I am sure that Fr. Quinlan was overly tired after celebrating all
those Masses. I understand the impatience with once-a-year visitors. As the only priest there, most of us don't know how he is able to minister to such a large number of people.

3. The accusation that Fr. Quinlan is a "brazen heretic." This is far from the truth. Fr. Quinlan does use "shock therapy" to get the attention of unbudgeable Catholics. But Fr. Quinlan is one of the most educated of our priests. In the opinion of many of his fellow priests, he is one of our best theologians and scripture experts. Even at the age of 75 and after 45 years of priestly ministry he still keeps up with the latest scholarship. He teaches a theology course every week with 100 to 150 parishioners in attendance; he is the most sought after Catholic priest for religious discussions at the local universities, in ecumenical settings, and for the adult formation sessions in many local parishes.
His quarterly lecture series brings in outstanding national speakers. The latest speaker had about 400 adults in attendance.

4. The TQ Notes: Most people call him " Father TQ" even though he lashes out against titles of any kind in our Church. He was extremely angry when Bishop Sullivan requested Rome to name some monsignors here. As indicated above, his major emphasis is education and formation of the modern day Catholic. With that in mind, he makes an effort not just to reach those who come weekly to his class or those who regularly attend Mass, but he periodically writes a column in his bulletin called "TQ's Notes." His parishioners go there first and then talk to each other over coffee after Mass about its content. I have included a copy of one of them.

Please let me know if you would like me to follow up on Mrs. Cabral's letter or want me to do anything more about this matter. I have not given Fr. Quinlan a copy of this letter. I will do so after hearing from you.

Sincerely yours in Christ,

(Rev. Msgr.) Thomas J. Caroluzza
Eastern Delegate of Cardinal Keeler

What's all the fuss about?

May 21, 2001

Pat O'Donnell
Church of the Holy Family
1279 N. Great Neck Rd.
Virginia Beach, VA 23454

Dear Mr. O'Donnell:

We have received calls of concern about the fish who are given away as prizes each year at the Church of the Holy Family annual fundraising fair and are writing to urge you to replace the fish with appropriate prize items for this year's fair.

Sadly, operators of these booths view the animals as expendable commodities and consider deaths due to inadequate handling and treatment a small cost of doing business. There is little or no instruction about the care of the fish given to those who "win" them and many suffer horribly and die before children can even get them home. In fact, fairgoers in past years report having seen children tossing the fish about haphazardly.

This casual attitude toward the welfare of these sentient animals sends the dangerous message to fairgoers that animals are disposable objects to be acquired and discarded on whim. The same irresponsible attitude has fueled the immense overpopulation crisis that results in millions of dogs and cats being killed in animal shelters every year. Children and adults alike should be taught compassion for animals, not sent the direct message that animals can and should be treated like fundraising tools.

We hope Church of the Holy Family will give this matter serious consideration and develop a policy prohibiting animal giveaways at all future fairs and other church events. May we hear from you? I can be reached at extension 1382 or by fax at 757-628-0781.

Sincerely,

Amy Rhodes
Cruelty Caseworker
Research, Investigations & Rescue Department

cc: Thomas J. Quinlan, Pastor
    Complainants

PeTA
PEOPLE FOR THE ETHICAL
TREATMENT OF ANIMALS

501 FRONT STREET
NORFOLK, VA 23510
TEL 757-622-PETA
FAX 757-622-0457

www.peta-online.org
info@peta-online.org

Church of the Holy Family

1279 N. Great Neck Road
Virginia Beach, VA 23454

June 6, 2001

Amy Rhodes
People for the Ethical Treatment of Animals
501 Front Street
Norfolk, Virginia 23510

Dear Ms. Rhodes

I waited until after our parish Fair was over before responding to your calumnious, judgemental, inane and arrogant letter of May 21, 2001.

1. You say you have received "calls of concern" about the fish we give as prizes at a certain booth. From whom? I receive questions and calls of concern about PETA's pressure tactics and strategies (sic) but none of us would respond to "certain" unidentified people.

2. You write: "Sadly, operators of these booths view the animals as expendable commodities." How could you possibly know that?? That is a' sin of calumny against human animals. You are totally out of ethical order. I spoke to many children nursing their "won" fish. They were concerned about getting their fish home quickly and giving them a new life, a veritable resurrection, since these particular fish were "predestined" as feeder fish to be killed by bigger fish.

3. You say our attitudes about these creatures is "casual". Prove it.

4. You state "that the casual attitude about the disposability of animals has caused an overpopulation of dogs and cats". That is the understatement of the new millennium! It is literally "raining cats and dogs" because of bizarre organizations like PETA. It is your unethical and casual attitude about human animals that is the greatest moral evil.

In the near future I plan to picket your cavalier attitude about children by having a few starving young-uns' standing in every DOG-FOOD, CAT-CHOW, POOPER-SCOOPER, LITTER-BOX aisle in all the local grocery stores, drawing attention to their plight and asking folks NOT to purchase these costly consumer products, thus allowing these creatures of God to die a natural and happy death.

Phone: (757) 481-5702
Fax: (757) 481-3989
Email: holyfamil1@aol.com
Website: http//members.aol.com/cothf/index.htm

Church of the Holy Family

1279 N. Great Neck Road
Virginia Beach, VA 23454

-2-

5. May I be of further help by suggesting that you and all the staff take a seminar in Franciscan/Creation (NOT Creationist!!!) Theology, that you might discover all the teachings of this facet of Catholic theology about spiritual substance, animal souls, Dog Heaven, etc. You are sorely in need of a new rationale for your mission????? We can provide it as it has been a teaching of our Church for almost 2,000 years; sc., that we MUST be compassionate, concerned, and nurturing towards all of God's creation.

6. Finally, I hereby cast a curse upon PETA: May the <u>GUSH EMUNIM</u> succeed in rebuilding the Third Temple in Jerusalem so that there will be the daily slaughtering of thousands of lambs, bullocks, and goats in worship. Then PETA can move its headquarters from 501 Front Street, Norfolk, Virginia, United States of America to 501 Holocaust Lane, Jerusalem, Israel.

That will be enough mission and work for all the PETA chapters of the world combined.

Yours - in Dogs, CAts and Fish,

T. Q.

(Rev.) Thomas J. Quinlan
Cruelty Caseworker for the Human Race

Phone: (757) 481-5702
Fax: (757) 481-3989
Email: holyfamil1@aol.com
Website: http//members.aol.com/cothf/index.htm

Ronald L. Ohrel, Jr.
3004 Sweet Cherry Circle
Virginia Beach, VA 23452

June 15, 2001

Most Rev. Walter F. Sullivan
Bishop of Richmond
811 Cathedral Place
Richmond, VA 23220

Dear Bishop Sullivan:

Enclosed please find copies of correspondence between Thomas J. Quinlan, Pastor of the Church of the Holy Family in Virginia Beach, and Amy Rhodes of the People for the Ethical Treatment of Animals. These letters were included in the June 9-10 parish bulletin.

I am also including a copy of my response to Fr. Quinlan.

I do not see how the written exchange could possibly be viewed as a positive example of how a Catholic should deal with conflict.

I must ask: what message was Fr. Quinlan trying to send to his congregation? Is this a person who can be counted on to give sound spiritual guidance?

Sincerely,

Ronald L. Ohrel, Jr.

enc

Office of the Bishop   *Diocese of Richmond*
811-B CATHEDRAL PLACE • RICHMOND, VIRGINIA 23220-4801 • (804) 359-5661

June 20, 2001

Reverend Thomas J. Quinlan
Holy Family Parish
1279 N. Great Neck Road
Virginia Beach, VA 23454

Dear T.Q.:

I just received the enclosed in the mail. I readily understand your response that you made to Amy Rhodes who is a member of the PETA organization.

Be assured of my full support. At the same time, may I suggest that you ignore rather than getting into the ring with such individuals on these particular subjects. Basically, it's a no win situation. Once you put something in writing, it is always there for someone to quote without mentioning any of the circumstances surrounding the reasons for your letter.

Best wishes.

Yours sincerely,

+ Walter F.

Walter F. Sullivan
Bishop of Richmond

ml

June 22, 2001

4 pages via fax: 804-358-9159
(hard copy to follow)

Most Reverend Bishop Walter F. Sullivan, D.D.
Bishop of Richmond
811 Cathedral Pl.
Richmond, VA 23220-4801

Dear Bishop Sullivan:

People for the Ethical Treatment of Animals (PETA) is an international nonprofit organization with more than 700,000 members dedicated to animal protection. In late May, we contacted the Church of the Holy Family, Parish #614, in Virginia Beach, after receiving calls of concern about a game booth at the church's annual fundraising fair at which live fish were to be given away as prizes. I have attached a copy of that letter for your review.

Also attached is a copy of Rev. Thomas J. Quinlan's response to our letter. As you can see, Rev. Quinlan's response is overtly hostile and unprofessional, to say the least. The tone of the letter indicates an obvious animosity toward PETA as well as toward members of the community (which include members of the parish) who have expressed concern about the practice of giving away live fish. The letter is disconcerting both because the issue at hand was obviously not given serious consideration and because its dismissive and acrimonious tone seems to run directly counter to the church's mission.

We have received numerous calls from parish members who are upset over what they believe to be inappropriate handling of this issue by Rev. Quinlan. One woman, whose father attends the church, apologized to me on behalf of the church. We are told that both letters are being circulated widely in the community, even at local hospitals.

We respectfully request that you address this matter as you deem appropriate. May we please hear from you? I can be reached at extension 1382 or by fax at 757-628-0781.

Sincerely,

Amy Rhodes, Cruelty Caseworker
Research, Investigations & Rescue Department

Attachments

PETA

PEOPLE FOR THE ETHICAL
TREATMENT OF ANIMALS

501 FRONT STREE
NORFOLK, VA 23510
TEL 757-622-PETA
FAX 757-622-045

www.peta-online.or
info@peta-online.org

Office of the Bishop
811-B CATHEDRAL PLACE • RICHMOND, VIRGINIA 23220-4801 • (804) 359-5661

Diocese of Richmond

June 29, 2001

Amy Rhodes
Cruelty Caseworker
501 Front Street
Norfolk, VA 23510

Dear Amy,

I received your letter in which you brought to my attention correspondence that you have had with Fr. Tom Quinlan, the Pastor of Holy Family Parish in Virginia Beach. I've also received some letters from people associated with PETA.

The correspondence is obviously between your organization and Fr. Quinlan. I am not taking sides to the situation nor am I defending the letter that you received from Fr. Quinlan.

Incidentally, I have three Schnauzers who receive the best of care. I certainly am supportive of the aims of your organization.

Thank you for writing.

Yours sincerely,

+Walter Sullivan
Walter F. Sullivan
Bishop of Richmond

July 4, 2001

Bishop Walter F. Sullivan
Bishop of Richmond
811-B Cathedral Place
Richmond, VA 23220-4801

Your Grace:

I read your letter to Ms. Rhodes. It is good to hear that you have schnauzers and we are thus encouraged that you are sensitive to the mistreatment of animals. That leads us to believe that when you say you are not taking a position against the casual give away of little fish by Father Tom Quinlan of the Holy Family Parish, or the rightness or wrongness of his scathingly unchristian letter to Ms. Rhodes, you are probably guiding Father Quinlan privately and quietly. That is, of course, none of our business and we will not enquire further.

There are, however, many who do look to you to make it clear that it is wrong to hurt animals needlessly. The reaction of Father Quinlan to a simple request to consider what happens to little fish, casually distributed at events, is disturbing for several reasons. Some members of his own congregation are upset but are fearful of "confronting" him because of his incredible bravado and apparent pride in sending out such a nasty missive.

As Bishop Desmond Tutu said: "If an elephant steps on a mouse's tail and you take no position, you have come out on the side of the oppressor." We know you have many matters to deal with, yet the disrespect for all life by a man of the cloth who was asked only to please consider being kind to animals, has caused more of a stir than you may know. We will leave it with you now.

Respectfully yours,

Ingrid E. Newkirk
President, PETA

James J. Martino
1504 Saybrook Cv.
Virginia Beach, VA 23464

June 28, 2001

Reverend Thomas J. Quinlan
Church of the Holy Family
1279 N. Great Neck Rd.
Virginia Beach, VA 23454

Dear Father Quinlan,

I was very disappointed to learn of your response to PETA's letter about the goldfish. As a Catholic, I am embarrassed for you that your response has become public. Your response was not something I would have expected from an educated man. It is certainly not something I would have expected from a moral leader in our community.

When your church received the letter from PETA, you became one of the thousands, perhaps hundreds of thousands of people to receive a letter from PETA reminding us to reach for a higher moral standard. I did not read the original letter that was sent to your church. Since I do not know exactly what it said, I must assume that it was quite offensive, given the tone of your response. Even if it was an all-out attack, which I doubt, I have higher expectations from our spiritual leaders. Or perhaps you were attacking PETA because of their reputation.

I was really disappointed when I saw Kerry Dougherty's column. It is unfortunate that in our society the attitude of our press is one of "if it bleeds, it leads." An organization such as PETA does so much good work, and often no one seems to care. No one shows up at press conferences, no one invites their spokespersons to be interviewed on the radio, and Kerry Dougherty doesn't write about them until they do something extreme or controversial.

The work done by the people at PETA is important. You and Ms. Dougherty may not respect or even like all their methods, but your attack was beneath the level of a leader. If you don't understand their work or their motives, I would like to invite you to join them one evening in the coldest part of the winter, as I did, to deliver a doghouse and straw (for free) to a "family dog" that isn't allowed in the house. A doghouse that was built with donated materials and delivered in the back of a volunteer's pickup truck. Imagine carrying this doghouse to the back corner of someone's property to find that the dog is in a 3x6' pen that doesn't even have a gate. The dog can never come out of his "prison-home." The family can't and doesn't want to get in. The dog's food is on the ground along with his feces. His water is in a 15-gallon pan that contains so much mud and feces that the water is brown, and it is frozen solid. Unfortunately, this dog isn't totally alone; in another corner of the yard, there is an even smaller pen, also with no gate, that has three smaller dogs in it. The dogs don't have 10 square feet to share. I have been there, and I have done it. I left in tears. There are people at PETA who do this kind of thing every day.

The next time you say mass, when you look down at your feet, wearing leather shoes, remember that your waist is tied with a leather belt. Adorned with the skin of tortured animals, are you truly giving glory to God? How can you praise God with a clear conscience when you're wearing misery? Have you risen to the highest moral level of which you are capable? Adam and Eve were not given permission to eat the animals, but mankind was not ready to live up to that high a standard. Mankind was not ready for Jesus, either, but he came and showed us a higher standard.

Every Easter, thousands and thousands of children are given rabbits and baby chickens. Most of these animals are doomed to a life of suffering. A life of loneliness. A life of neglect. Animal support organizations ask parents not to give these animals to children, because they know that it is a sentence to a short, harsh life for these animals. Unfortunately, too many parents do not realize this. There are easy profits to be made on the sale of these "cheap" and "expendable" animals.

Then someone notices that a church fair is giving away goldfish as prizes and asks PETA to say something. Oftentimes, something that seems harmless on the surface really isn't. Just as often, the leaders involved don't notice the small things. Sometimes the little things need to be pointed out. These goldfish are not necessarily predestined to be "feeder fish," as you stated. They are raised specifically for easy sale at a high profit margin. Take a walk through a pet store and look at all the sick fish in the fish tanks. The profit margins are so high that most pet stores don't care about the losses due to death. If it weren't for the extreme profit margins, they wouldn't have been bred in the first place. And as far as being a feeder fish, there is a big difference in being part of the food chain that God set up in nature and being cruelly manipulated by mankind.

I have too often heard criticism of people for making an effort to help the animals when there are more deserving causes. Indeed, I myself have received such criticism. Am I a sinner because I don't spend my time and money working for the Heart Association? Or maybe the American Cancer Society is a better cause, so I should give my time and money to it? Or maybe the best charity is the battered women's shelter. Am I a sinner because I didn't choose what others consider the very best cause? I suppose we should all give our time and money to what the majority has decided to be the single best cause and let all the others dwindle away. Is only the single best cause deserving of our efforts? No, obviously we are better off because we each can follow our own path and support a cause that has special meaning to us. Instead of criticizing these people at PETA who give from the depth of their soul to something they believe in, try to be the moral standard your parishioners look up to. Rise to your highest level. Push your followers to rise up to their highest level. Animal rights may not be your cause of choice, but how could you vilify someone who is working to protect the least of God's creatures? I ask you once again, Father Quinlan, if He were here today, just what would Jesus do?

Yours in Christ,

James Martino

Church of the Holy Family

1279 N. Great Neck Road
Virginia Beach, VA 23454

August 17, 2001

Dear Mr. Martino:

It has taken me a long time to answer all the letters and email that have co.me in. You are the last one, at least for now.

Thank you for your interest and comments.

However, there are so many assumptions and subsumptions in your letter it is diffiuclt to know where to begin.

I am sorry taht you are embarrassed "for" me. It is the exact kind of a letter you should ahve expected.

You You attribute to PETA something it does not have - a higher moral standard. WE have the highest moral standard and it comes from the Gospel. IN fact, PETA doesn't avhe a rational or moral basis they can articulate.

PETA does a lot of good work. I agree. PETA does a lot of bad work. Most agree.

People are forever abusing people, animals and insects throughout the history of the human race. This is a result of the original defect (Cf. Genesis, Chapters 1 - 11). But neither you nor PETA nor the Church can do away with that. All we can do is to be and encourage others to be FREELy compassioante towards all of God's Creation. Sin is here to stay. And Grace, taht can overcome it when free-will people respond is also here to stay. IF Jesus didnt' get rid of sin, neither will you, or PETA. That's the excitment of being alive. Being free. Being filled with Grace that can overcome sin and evil. You can't wipe it out.

For every cat and dog and love-bird story of yorus, I have fifty more of cruelty to children.

"Prove it" was meant to covney to the leaders of PETA that they were making judgements instead of stating facts. It is their lack of logic and common-sense that is to pitiful.

Yes, Jesus ahs asked us to rise above the former ways of the race. He has asked us to transform the world - with jsutice, equity, and compassion.

When anyone kills an animal or fish for food they should do so in

Phone: (757) 481-5702
Fax: (757) 481-3989
Email: holyfamil1@aol.com
Website: http//members.aol.com/cothf/index.htm

Church of the Holy Family

1279 N. Great Neck Road
Virginia Beach, VA 23454

-2-

the mnost humane way. That is Jewish/Christian teaching. PETA didn't invent that concept.

Animal testing is not obsolete as you erroneously presume. You too, who claim to be a Christian, need a course in Franciscan theology, just one part of our multi-branched spiritualities. Tell PETA to do its homework. Read them the story of The tAmed Wolf of Gubbio from ST. Francis "Little Flowers of ST. Francis".

What text are you citing to document that ADam and EVe were not given permission to eat animals . THE ELEPHANT ate the gcazelle and them gazelle ate the dog and the dog ate the fly, adn teh fly ate the amoeba. What planet are you on. And all God-designed!!!

Bunnies and chickens at EAster. Great symbols. The ones that are treated badlyk. That is a problem of parenting. INcidentall butterflies are the best symbol for cAtholics. I don't know if you can eat them.

You are constantly using an illogical arguemnt. It is called PROPERT QUOD, ERGO QUOD = Such and such is presumed true, and thil is the result". The only problem is your result doesn't follow from its protesis.

You asked me twice: WHAT WOULD JESU,S DO? The real Jesus would go to the Temple whenver he could get there and pray and offer (and watch) thousands of sheep, lambs, goats, and birds have their throats slit and the blood poured out on the horns of the high altar. What the hell else would you expect Him to do????

Maybe I'll send you a new T-shirt "JESUS LOVED TO EAT FISH, ESPECIALLY AFTER THE RESURRECTION"."

Sincerely,

T, Q

(Rev.) Thomas J. Quinlan

Phone: (757) 481-5702
Fax: (757) 481-3989
Email: holyfamil1@aol.com
Website: http//members.aol.com/cothf/index.htm

Thank God! PETA has finally met its match

KERRY DOUGHERTY

It's finally happened. After hassling Burger King, McDonald's, Vogue Magazine and cancer-stricken New York City Mayor Rudy Giuliani, PETA has met its match.

When the militant bunny-huggers launched a broadside against a Beach church for a goldfish giveaway at a fair this spring, they may have thought they were taking on a country curate. A reticent reverend. A turn-the-other-cheek Christian chump.

Instead, they crossed swords with the outspoken, chain-smoking Rev. Tom Quinlan — just call him TQ — pastor of the Church of the Holy Family in Virginia Beach.

In response to PETA's attack on the goldfish prizes, Quinlan anointed himself "Cruelty Caseworker to the Human Race" and unleashed a blistering counter-attack filled with something missing from PETA's barrage: logic, and compassion — for people.

"I had never thought much about PETA before," Quinlan confessed when I called him this week after a proud parishioner delivered a copy of his letter to my house. "But I could hardly believe the level of their arrogance."

It began on May 21 with a typical PETA screed sent to the carnival chairman of Quinlan's church. In it, Amy Rhodes, PETA "Cruelty Caseworker," claimed that the animal rights group had received "calls of concern" about the welfare of goldfish that were given away at the Holy Family church fair.

Rhodes fired off the usual sanctimonious PETA-prattle, accusing others of a casual attitude toward "sentient" animals and scolding the church for distributing the little fish. The inane epistle brought a whole new meaning to the word "carping."

She closed the letter with a cursory "May we hear from you?"

Be careful what you ask for, Ms. Rhodes.

TQ immediately went on the offensive, penning a brilliant response replete with theology, deontology, ichthyology — and even a curse.

Dear Ms. Rhodes, I waited until after our parish fair was over before responding to your calumnious, judgmental, inane and arrogant letter.

Calumnious — it doesn't get much better than that.

TQ then vivisected PETA's high-handed letter bit by bit.

You write: "Sadly operators of these booths view the animals as expendable commodities." How could you possibly know that? That is a sin of calumny against human animals. You are totally out of ethical order.

You go, Father.

In response to PETA's assertion that a "casual attitude about the disposability of animals" abounds at church

Please see **Dougherty,** *Page* **B2**

Dougherty: Pastor wants common sense from animal defenders

Continued from Page B1

carnivals, Quinlan demanded that Rhodes "prove it" before letting loose with a searing attack on PETA's callous attitude toward humans.

In the near future I plan to picket your cavalier attitude about children by having a few starving young-uns standing in every dog food, cat food, pooper-scooper and litter box aisle in all the local grocery stores, drawing attention to their plight and asking folks not to purchase these costly consumer products thus allowing these creatures of God to die a natural and happy death.

(And the good reverend probably didn't even know that PETA has been waging a relentless campaign against the March of Dimes, trying to pressure corporations to stop supporting the charity that works tirelessly to stamp out birth defects. PETA is outraged because sometimes saving children from a lifetime of misery involves animal research.)

Quinlan pointed out that before lecturing church folks about goldfish, PETA might want to study Catholic teachings that direct the faithful to be *compassionate, concerned and nurturing towards all of God's creation.*

He saved the best for last, of course:

Finally, I hereby cast a curse upon PETA: May the Gush Emunim succeed in rebuilding the Third Temple in Jerusalem so that there will be the daily slaughtering of thousands of lambs, bullocks, and goats in worship.

Quinlan postulated that such an animal holocaust would force PETA to uproot from Norfolk and move to Israel.

"That part was tongue-in-cheek, of course," Quinlan told me of his good wishes toward the Israeli fundamendalists.

So far, the silence from 501 Front St. in Norfolk has been deafening.

"What can they possibly say?" Quinlan asked, laughing. "I'm right."

Score one for the Cruelty Caseworker for the Human Race.

■ *Reach Kerry at 446-2306 or at kerry.dougherty@att.net*

OBJECTION!

Don't be cruel to PETA: Find some other (gold)fish to fry

These letters are in response to Kerry Dougherty's June 23 column, "Thank God! PETA has finally met its match":

Fish don't belong at a church fair

Has Kerry Dougherty ever met an animal she didn't dislike? She sneered at the PETA letter that asked a congregation to nix its fish-in-a-Gladbag giveaway, calling it an "inane epistle."

What does Ms. Dougherty think fish are? Toys that kids can tote around on carnival rides? Fish are living, breathing creatures that need oxygen to sustain life.

Those baggies hold just so much water, just so much oxygen. It isn't right that fish should be bounced around at a church bazaar. I'm with PETA on this one.

Beth Rosenberg
Chesapeake

Indifferent to cruelty, if it spoils the fun

What do circus-going parents say to animal advocates protesting outside? "How could you ruin it for the children?"

What do they say when you try to teach kids that being an animal on ol' McDonald's farm is the last thing any animal wants to be? "How could you scare the children?"

And, more recently, how do they respond when you say selling fish in plastic bags is not only dangerous for the fish, it conveys a message that animals are mere playthings to be bought like so many sticks of cotton candy? They call you "calumnious, judgmental and arrogant." And their cheerleaders chime in with "Score one for the Cruelty Caseworker for the Human Race."

Are you catching the drift here? When you're dealing with people who don't care about animals, their discussion never centers on the main point — the animals being exploited. It's always about them being bothered by your attempt to thwart their fun.

Lynda Cozart
Chesapeake

Fish are one of God's creatures, not a trinket

My jaw dropped as I read Kerry Dougherty's piece praising the Rev. Tom Quinlan's silly letter to PETA.

It isn't unreasonable to believe that goldfish are not commodities and deserve not to be treated as such. PETA is right — giving away live fish as if they are trinkets just begs for abuse. People don't go to a fair expecting to come home with a goldfish. I'm sure many of these poor fish suffered in the heat, and after they got home to, what, a hastily assembled home in a bucket of water?

It would be nice if the good reverend could dismount from his high horse long enough to realize that PETA's request had merit, and that they are guilty only of wanting to protect animals — a worthy goal.

As Jesus said, "As you do to the least of them, so you do to me."

Harriet Avery
Virginia Beach

Misquoting the Bible is no blessing for animals

In her usual animal-unfriendly stance, Kerry Dougherty sidles up (this time) with a reverend. If this religious collusion was sought as an attempt to gain celestial strength to her case, she can forget it.

Five years ago, I viewed three gut-wrenching videos of the warehouse-like conditions of "factory farms." When my family got together the next time, we discussed what I had learned and decided we could all do something to help correct the animals' plight.

Four of my relatives agreed to no longer buy meat, basing the decision on their ethical belief systems. The only holdout was my sister — the religious one — who said she wouldn't give it up "because the Bible said we have dominion over the animals."

How many acts of cruelty have been dismissed using this misinterpreted missive? Too many to count.

Robert J. English
Chesapeake

A poor example for young readers

Kerry Dougherty's scathing, mocking remarks in the end support the exploitation of animals for fun and profit.

Young adults form judgments based on the "wise" writings they read in newspapers. It is a very disturbing thought that she could conceivably sway future generations into believing, as she does, that there is no level of animal suffering that isn't justified if it is endured for the sake of humanity.

Dennis Wise
Virginia Beach

Ganging up on PETA

Kerry Dougherty's column was a slavish glorification of an inane and buffoonish letter written by her fellow PETA-hater, the Rev. Tom Quinlan.

The Dougherty-Quinlan tag team takes the nonsensical position that people who are concerned about the mistreatment of the other feeling creatures who share our world are somehow guilty of not caring about humans. Ms. Dougherty considers the Rev. Quinlan's trite blather to be "brilliant." I consider it to be sophomoric and pathetic.

Randolph D. Stowe
Norfolk

Unconventional reverend should be a kindred spirit

Kerry Dougherty says PETA has met its match in the Rev. Tom Quinlan and she is right — the Rev. Quinlan has a knack for grabbing attention and stirring up controversy that makes some of our more "outrageous" stunts pale by comparison.

According to a Pilot news article from last year, the Rev. Quinlan has a "fat" file at the Vatican, full of complaints about his unorthodox way of doing things, including carting church statues off to the city dump and calling children worried about his smoking habit, "brainwashed little suburban monsters."

One would think such a rebel would see a kindred spirit in PETA — from lobbing tofu cream pies to going naked instead of wearing fur, we will do just about anything to get the word out about animal cruelty.

However, unlike the Rev. Quinlan, we think there's room in this world for compassion for all who suffer, from hungry children to hungry dogs and cats, to goldfish given away like balloons at fairs.

Many prizes would delight children that don't involve exposing animals to mistreatment and neglect. All we ask is that the church opt for prizes that don't die if dropped off a carnival ride or if left, forgotten, in a car.

Amy Rhodes
Cruelty caseworker, PETA
Norfolk

Be grateful for PETA's caring and rescue skills

In the five years I've been in this area, I've read a lot of negative press about PETA. However, I'm grateful they're here.

Two years ago, two piebilled grebes became entangled in landscape netting that somehow found its way into a lake. It was cutting into their necks, their heads through the grids with the line stretched between their bills like a gag. Their wings were tangled so that flight was impossible.

PETA's rescue department came out and managed to get the birds, cut the netting off and get them to a wildlife rehabilitator, where they were treated and later released successfully.

More recently, a young duck lost a leg to what we think was a turtle attack. Again, PETA came within 1½ hours of my call and rescued the duck.

PETA assists in rescues with skill, enthusiasm and a deep concern for the animal. We are fortunate to have this organization in our area.

Sherry L. Marchy
Chesapeake

Office of the Bishop — Diocese of Richmond
811-B CATHEDRAL PLACE • RICHMOND, VIRGINIA 23220-4801 • (804) 359-5661

July 2, 2001

Rev. Thomas J. Quinlan
Holy Family Parish
1279 N. Great Neck Road
Virginia Beach, VA 23454

Dear TQ,

Bill Pitt sent to me the article by Kerry Dougherty in the <u>Virginian Pilot</u> entitled "Thank God! PETA has finally met its match".

Congratulations! You certainly received a rounding letter of support. Your friend, Mrs. Rhodes, of PETA did write to me and I guess she wanted me to respond to your letter to PETA. I took the coward way out by saying that I would not get involved in correspondence between you and Mrs. Rhodes.

Congratulations!! The article in the paper is truly excellent and well deserved.

Yours sincerely,

Walter F. Sullivan
Bishop of Richmond

Office of the Bishop
811-B CATHEDRAL PLACE • RICHMOND, VIRGINIA 23220-4801 • (804) 359-5661

Diocese of Richmond

September 17, 2001

Reverend Thomas Quinlan
Holy Family Parish
1279 N. Great Neck Road
Virginia Beach, VA 23454-2117

Dear T.Q.:

Enclosed is an article that appeared in a recent issue of The Tablet.

At the next parish bazaar, instead of having gold fish you need to have little turtles and set up your own gambling casino.

Enjoy.

Yours sincerely,

Walter F. Sullivan
Bishop of Richmond

ml
Encl.

Beached turtles

IN MARCH the Archbishop of Cincinnati, Daniel Pilarczyk, sent a reminder to his parish clergy. Last year, he recalled, he had told them that it was not appropriate to use live animals in gambling at church festivals. Parishes should "mirror the compassion of Jesus" by not inflicting pain on animals.

Animal rights activists, of course, are delighted at the archbishop's intervention. But pity Fr James Shappelle, priest at St Bernard's in the tree-lined Cincinnati suburb of Winton Place, who this year ended his church's turtle derbies after 26 years. How does a turtle derby work? "People bet 50 cents on their favourite turtle. At the beginning of the race the turtles are given a little nudge", Fr Shappelle explains. "The one who crosses the line first, that's the winner."

Far from being cruel, he says the 25 turtles the church used to order from a laboratory in Wisconsin were later released into a small pond where they grew in number. This year his parish festival, *sans* turtles, brought in only $500 – compared with $5,000 last year. Far fewer people came, says Fr Shappelle. "They missed the turtles."

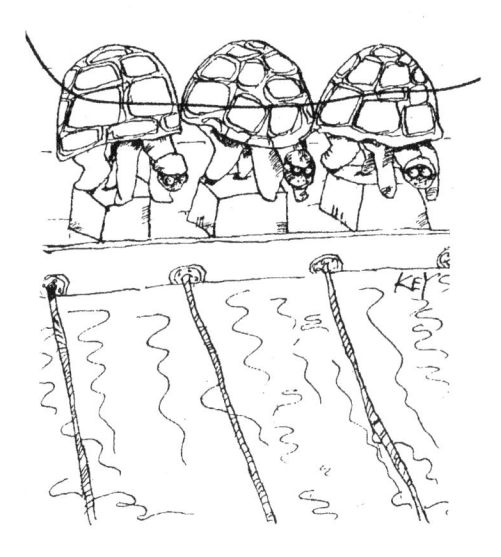

In defiance of the Archbishop of Cincinnati, Turtles for a Changing Church have held their annual race

ON, TO THE NEXT ADVENTURE!

Come Celebrate Our "Retirement"!

The end of an era: A brand new Day!

An invitation to say Good-Bye:

From

Rev. Mgsr. Thomas J. Caroluzza

Rev. John J. Dorgan

Rev. Mgsr. William L. Pitt

Rev. Thomas J. Quinlan

Sunday, June 5, 2005 1:00 - 3:00 p.m.

Philippine Cultural Center
4857 Baxter Road, Virginia Beach, VA 23462

Directions: I-64E; exit Independence to Princess Anne; exit Baxter Road.

NOT FOR PUBLICATION UNTIL, ON OR AFTER JUNE 13, 2005

A Pastor's Forced Retirement

Week of June13, 2005
ESSAYS IN THEOLOGY
By Rev. Richard P. McBrien

Social scientists have made studies of the behavior of diocesan bishops, observing how important answering their mail is to so many of them. Perhaps it is because the process is easily quantified, yielding a clear sense of accomplishment at day's end.

Many of these same bishops, however, are also vulnerable to undue pressure from the disgruntled.

Anyone familiar with written exchanges between bishops and laity know that bishops have standard ways of putting off complaints from the left, but their responses to complaints from the right are of ,a different sort, especially in the current ecclesiastical climate.

In early March, the bishop of an East-coast diocese received a detailed complaint from an individual who "just happened" to attend Mass in one of its parishes. The pastor also "just happened" to be one of the best known and most controversial priests in the diocese.

The complainer, who lives in a neighboring diocese, was appalled by the celebration of the Eucharist on that particular Sunday. He objected to the homily, to the form of the Eucharistic Prayer that was used, to the absence of kneelers in the church, to the pastor's invitation to the whole congregation to join in the proclaiming of the doxology at the end of the Eucharistic Prayer, and to the fact that the pastor left the altar at the "Our Father" to join hands in prayer with those in the first row.

Not surprisingly, the letter's language was redolent of another era in U.S. Catholic history. Its sanctimonious and self-righteous tone was exceeded only by its obvious determination to "do in" the pastor.

The writer assured the bishop, whom he always addressed as "Your Excellency," that he was a member "in good standing" of his home parish. How many Catholics nowadays would have felt the need to add that superfluous phrase?

He also insisted that he was writing only "after deep prayer and reflection." He made this point again toward the end of the letter, adding the phrase, "for several weeks." I would guess that more than half the priests in the diocese would roll their eyes over those lines.

The writer consistently referred to the Eucharist as the "sacred" Mass, as if the Mass were anything but sacred. The Church was not simply "the Church" but "our universal Mother Church."

He informed the bishop that he did not take Communion because the Mass that had been celebrated that morning was, for him, "invalid and a sacrilege." He reported returning to his home parish that evening where he "attended a true sacred mass."

He assured the bishop that he would "continue to pray" for the pastor and his parishioners (more rolling of eyes from the pastor's brother priests) and that "Our Lord Jesus Christ, who is Our Hope and Our Light, may bless each of us and keep us always as one, holy, Catholic and apostolic Church in His tender care."

This letter would ordinarily not merit even a mention here. However, only two weeks later a diocesan official wrote to the pastor, at the bishops's request, seeking a formal response to the accusations.

The pastor answered each item in the complaint. Five days later, he met with the bishop, and three days after that was informed that he was being removed as pastor–only a month after this whole process had begun.

Needless to say, his many hundreds of parishioners have been shocked and upset by the bishop's decision. For all of his unconventional behavior, this pastor is genuinely loved by the great majority of his people. I have been there. I have seen it for myself.

It is an unusually active and vibrant parish, where every member is expected to engage in a ministry of one kind or another. No Sunday-only Catholics there.

Seven years ago, on the 40th anniversary of the pastor's ordination, the previous bishop composed an Ode to him, referring to the pastor as "the Blue Angel." In that Ode, the bishop remarked on the priest's "tireless care of the poor, the sick, the old, and the lame."

For 40 years, he said, the pastor "had preached and labored...to make Jesus, the Gospel, and our faith take on new life for us."

He even compared him to St. Peter, who was praised, but also mocked. "But just like Simon Peter, [his] love for all God's people is solid as a rock."

The bishop called him a "faithful, ageless, and glorious priest."

But not according to the ultra-conservative letter-writer, whose complaint to the new bishop trumped all else.

This week's column is dedicated to this pastor, known to many as simply TQ.

©2005 Richard P. McBrien. All rights reserved. Fr. McBrien is the Crowley-O'Brien Professor of Theology at the University of Notre Dame.

Made in the USA
San Bernardino, CA
10 May 2014